I0884874

CHRISTIAN LANGUAGE IN THE SECULAR CITY

These are sermons of intense feeling, but they invite us not to explorations of our individual sentiments but to a sensing of the truths exposed – 'classical' truths of Christian faith. They deserve repeated pondering and savouring. I am profoundly thankful that there are such 'classical' voices for us to hear in the contemporary church. Without them, what we say is going to be less than adequate to the complex and exhilarating realities of God and humanity.
The Most Reverend Dr Rowan Williams, Archbishop of Wales

This is a rich and stimulating set of sermons. David Martin has the tact, insight and learning to repristimate ancient tradition and apply it – with good humour and sharpness – to the ordinarinesses and strangenesses of life.
John Drury, Dean of Christ Church, Oxford, UK

Christian Language in the Secular City offers a series of meditations by the internationally renowned sociologist, David Martin. Martin presents a distinctive angle of vision on key issues of Christian faith, dividing the book into three clear sections: the Liturgical Year; the Christian agenda, including prophecy, justification, sacred places and spaces, wisdom, providence, peace and war, angelic and demonic; and Emergent Occasions such as the fall of the Berlin Wall, the 900th anniversary of Winchester Cathedral, commemoration of the poets and martyrs, and more.

With its uniquely lyrical presentation, David Martin's book transposes central issues of theology and Christian faith into a new key. This book complements David Martin's theoretical book focusing on *Christian Language and its Mutations*, published in Ashgate's *Religion and Society in Interdisciplinary Perspective* series.

David Martin is Honorary Professor in the Department of Religious Studies, Lancaster University, and Emeritus Professor of Sociology at the London School of Economics, UK. He is the author of some two dozen books, including *Divinity in a Grain of Bread*, and many landmark titles in the sociology of religion.

For Bernice
with love and gratitude for these forty years

Christian Language in the Secular City

DAVID MARTIN
Lancaster University and
London School of Economics

Routledge
Taylor & Francis Group
LONDON AND NEW YORK

First published 2002 by Ashgate Publishing

Reissued 2018 by Routledge
2 Park Square, Milton Park, Abingdon, Oxon OX14 4RN
711 Third Avenue, New York, NY 10017, USA

Routledge is an imprint of the Taylor & Francis Group, an informa business

Typeset by Manton Typesetters, Louth, Lincolnshire, UK.

A Library of Congress record exists under LC control number: 2002100378

ISBN 13: 978-1-138-73383-1 (hbk)
ISBN 13: 978-1-138-73382-4 (pbk)
ISBN 13: 978-1-315-18701-3 (ebk)

So to explain what it means to Christians to say that God is a fountain of living water, or a vine-keeper, or a rock or a fortress, or king requires an account not merely of fountains, rocks, vines and kings but of a whole tradition of experiences and of the literary tradition which records and interprets them.

Janet Soskice, *Metaphor and Religious Language*, Oxford: Clarendon, 1985, Chapter 10, p. 158.

The 'teaching songs', which the women teachers were reciting [in the fourth century Syrian Church] ... consisted in poetic meditations on the symbols and types which God distributed in nature and scripture to lead people across the chasm separating creatures from their Creator. For Ephraem's theology is not propositional but typological and symbolic. The symbols and types are not esoteric but commonplace ... within the Bible, the Gospel is the exegetical focal point; all the figures ultimately point to Christ. For Ephraem the symbols and types are so many verbal icons, and his thought is not so much theology as it is a sacramental iconology ... Ephraem's thought is Semitic rather than Hellenic, flowing almost directly from the discourse of the scriptures rather than commenting on them.

Sidney Griffith 'The Eucharist as "Living Medicine"', in Sarah Beckwith (ed.), *Catholicism and Catholicity: Eucharistic Communities in Historical and Contemporary Perspectives*, Oxford: Blackwell, 1999, pp. 115–16.

A hunger-bitten and idea-less philosophy naturally produces a starveling and comfortless religion. It is among the miseries of the present age that it recognises no medium between Literal and Metaphorical.

S.T. Coleridge, *Lay Sermons*, pp. 40–42, quoted in Richard Holmes *Coleridge, Darker Reflections* 1998, p. 441

Contents

Foreword

The word 'classical' provokes mixed emotions. It can mean little more than 'well-worn'; it can, in architecture, suggest a rather formal and chilly style. But at least it has, in common use, some association with the idea of the sort of excellence that establishes lasting standards.

David Martin's preaching voice is, I believe, 'classical' in several senses. It is never chilly, but it does what the classical voice in literature always strives to do – to open up the depths of feeling without simply indulging individual dramas and sensations. These are sermons of intense feeling, but they invite us not to explorations of our individual sentiments but to a sensing of the truths exposed. And those truths are the 'classical' truths of Christian faith. The sermons here presented are unmistakeably contemporary, but equally unmistakeably free from up-to-the-minute polemic or simply journalistic comment. They set the events and experiences of today in the immeasurable context of the nature and action of the eternal God, made known in Jesus Christ. They are a cleansing of our vision, a stilling of our restless itch to solve the problems of our environment whether we have the resources or not – an itch more to do with anxiety than charity. In that sense they also enable truthful and loving response to the world, with our illusions well chastened.

So they are classical too in outlining what a good sermon might be: clearly focussed on God, both enlarging and sobering our imagination, moving us to repentance and to expectancy, helping us celebrate the scope and the beauty of the world that revelation reveals. These sermons deserve repeated pondering and savouring. I am profoundly thankful that there are such 'classical' voices for us to hear in the contemporary Church. Without them, what we say is going to be less than adequate to the complex and exhilarating realities of God and humanity.

Rowan Williams, Archbishop of Wales

Preface

The addresses in this book continue from an earlier collection *Divinity in a Grain of Bread* published in 1989 by Lutterworth, and complement my *The Breaking of the Image* published in 1980 by Blackwell and *Does Christianity Cause War* published in 1997 by Oxford University Press, especially Chapters 5 and 6. Most were given in Guildford Cathedral and I thank the Dean, the Very Revd Alex Wedderspoon, for that privilege and for his constant encouragement. The rest were given in various places: St Edward's, Cambridge (The Commemoration of Reformation Martyrs); Little St Mary's, Cambridge; Christ's College, Cambridge; Oriel College, Oxford; Winchester Cathedral (a 900th anniversary occasion attended by the County Council); St Peter's, Old Woking (Restoration); St Alfege, Greenwich; St Michael's, Cornhill; The Temple Church, London, and St Hilda and St Bede, Durham University. One or two were once in a lifetime occasions as when I spoke at Guildford on 'The Remembrance of Things Past' following the fall of the Berlin Wall. The address on the Resurrection commemorates Christopher Gray, murdered in the course of his priestly duties, and the final address commemorates my friend Donald Davie.

Preface

Introduction

Banner 10 – The Transfiguration

Taken from *The Creation: The Banners of Winchester Cathedral* by Thetis Blacker, Friends of Winchester Cathedral, 2001.

Introduction

These addresses, originally composed in response to the lectionary and the liturgical year, as well as 'emergent occasions', are presented as a way of doing theology much more as part of worship than as philosophical argument. They are, therefore, invocatory and seek to evoke according to the classical model in hymn, scripture, sermon and painting. That model rearranges and juxtaposes quotations in a way that stirs up resonances. The sermon is plagiaristic just as the gospels are by using what is already incised on the tablets of the heart in fresh combinations and senses. That is one reason why I make no attempt to identify the numerous glancing quotations embedded in the text.

Because theology can be seen as an angle of vision in the course of constant re-vision (but not successive displacement) it is also fragmentary, just as Pascal's *Pensées* are fragmentary. You cannot say everything all at once but have to find out directions by indirections. It also happens to be the case that I personally am not equipped to write a formal treatise, so I have an interest in emphasizing the way integrated form can distort richness of content. But how can you possibly catch the multiple reflections and the infinity of meanings embedded in the tiniest fragment of gospel by reducing them to a linear argument or a treatise – valid though such modes are in their own terms?

In suggesting that theology is invocation and evocation, calling upon and calling out, one is not trying to render it immune to philosophical critique as a discourse *sui generis*. After all, even music, the most invocatory and evocative of human activities, can be subjected to philosophical criticism. My point is that theology understood as a poetry of transfiguration (and so, also of deformation) is not easily treated as a discourse of formal logic or empirical connection. If the latter were the case then it would be verifiable and falsifiable, and nothing more nor less than science. Unless one holds the Christian mode to be merely pre-scientific and obsolete, one has to understand what kinds of connection it exemplifies. To put it another way, one has to elucidate the alternative logic that informs Bible, hymn, patristic writers, the sermon and Christian iconography. In the sermon one is looking for the verbal equivalents of what roused so much curiosity in the National Gallery exhibition 'Seeing Salvation'. One needs to *hear* salvation and not attempt the impossible and reductionist task of forcing so-called 'modern' meanings out of images and texts through demythologization. Demythologization is a modern myth.

The logic of theology in this mode is not a free-for-all dependent on successive shakes of the kaleidoscope of images but rather congruences and typological cross references growing organically out of a fundamental thematic repertoire. In my own thinking that repertoire derives from the relation between vision and 'the world' in the manner set out in Max Weber's essay 'Religious Rejections of the World and their Direction'. Thus to whatever degree Christianity, Islam and Judaism may share common elements, such as monotheism, their angles on 'the world' are quite distinctive. Our world visions differ according to a quite limited set of possible angles. The task of theology then, as I understand it, is to uncover the developmental potential of the Christian repertoire, what it positively implies and negatively constrains, with a particular normative reference to the developments and directions initially embedded in the New Testament.

Of course, there is room for individual variations on the basic themes, just as there is room for distinctive harmonizations in music, but at the same time the personal element is being tested against historic correspondences and understood linkages, and against a rule of faith. One probes what is handed down – tradition – to rework its sense within the outer constraints of the rule. Given that any such sense includes contradiction one is committed to probing paradox and holding together truths rather than rendering them blandly complementary. It is, for example, simultaneously a rule of faith that God is beyond all we can imagine and yet his nature and his name are known in the express image of a human face. Again, God is universally present yet his 'real presence' is realized in particular times and places, as on Mount Horeb or the Mount of Transfiguration.

Testing against deeply embedded correspondences and against an orthodoxy is not at all submission to arbitrary authority. One has to have strong guidelines to think at all and to be intelligible to others, yet one also tries to be both liberal and catholic, taking every kind of critical pressure into account and (in Max Weber's sense) seeing 'how much one can bear'. For a long time I used Montefiore's commentaries on the gospels because they were so antithetical to my own thinking. Enlightened method makes non-sense of the gospel because it imagines it can pluck the heart out of its mystery when, in fact, it glides helplessly over the surface. 'Critical method' is a major achievement, but once one has absorbed what it has to offer, one turns to the kind of profound commentary found in Hopkins, Eliot, Auden, Emily Dickinson and above all, so far as I am concerned, the writing of John Ruskin as collected by Mary and Ellen Gibbs in *The Bible References of John Ruskin* (1898). Once you have fished on one side of the boat you have to fish for richer fry on the other.

John Drury is a contemporary who engages in this style of thinking, not only because he sees the gospels as written by artists reworking a complex code of cross-related signs, but in his remarkable elucidations of that same code in medieval and renaissance painting. Moreover, in its actual use as distinct from its complex elaboration, the code is profoundly democratic, because the simplest believer has been saturated in its images, incarnations and embodiments, not in free-floating concepts and notions. Indeed, 'belief' and this saturation are intimately related. A hymn by Wesley is powerful and widely appealing just because it creatively reworks all the familiar connections. Christian language is known and responded to in its use, not through extraneous explanation. (And, of course, saturation is above all powerful with respect to the Authorised Version and the *Book of Common Prayer.*[1])

Another resource in returning to the common typological method of the gospels and the Church is Northrop Frye's *The Great Code*. In that inexhaustible book he sets out the scriptural types and antitypes, which have historically also been richly cross-referenced against classical mythology, though today we dare not use those particular cross-references. (I have also been greatly helped by *The Literary Guide to the Bible* (1987) edited by Frank Kermode and Robert Alter.)

At any rate, one takes the Scripture as it is, and early Christianity as an accelerating development of fertile seeds, without assuming that everything turns on speculations, often theologically driven, about what is most primitive. Thus Geza Vermes's profound excavations concerning Jesus the Jew in no way prevent one attending to the growth of the original 'mustard seeds' as normative for Christianity. It would also be a salutary exercise to set all the varied 'assured results' in parallel columns like an ancient harmony of the gospels in reverse to see just how much and how little was absolutely out and absolutely in.

Typological method is akin to anthropological structuralism and one can very quietly employ both together. It seems to me, contrary to a great deal of received opinion, that the overall tenor of the New Testament is singularly clear, and internally coherent, if you do not attempt to stretch it on an alien rack. Thus a Lucan saying about the humble being exalted complements the sayings in Ephesians and John to the effect that 'He that descended is also he that ascended', which is the governing pattern of the creed itself and the whole theology of 'condescension' and reversal. What one might call the upper and the lower levels of reference complement each other, just as the incarnation complements the centrality of the child in the kingdom.

There are links with sociology as well as anthropology. I have suggested (in my *Reflections on Sociology and Theology*, 1997, and in a recently prepared companion volume on *Christian Language and its Mutations*), that what in sociology is presented in terms of extended empirical observation is in theology an impacted and poetic concentrate inviting embodiment and enactment. Both disciplines share a subject matter of exiles and restorations, migrations to promised lands and new orders, borders closed to protect vision and borders opened to make it universally available, the blood ties of tribe and family set over against spiritual brotherhood and sisterhood, the inwardness of conscience set over against the necessary constraint of the law, the equality before God set against the necessary mediations of embedded authority.

In these addresses I try to rework the language of Christianity in relation to such themes as the pressure and fulfilment of time; embodiments of divinity in the human form and in the compressed action of the Eucharist; the conversion of the temple into a fraternity and a universal 'body'; Jerusalem as the site for ideal visions of peace and spirals of violence and expulsion; angelic messages in relation to demonic bedevilments and dis-eases; rebirths and transformations; sacred wisdom and divine folly; real presences and real absences; repeated remissions and renewed demands.

All these reflect the concerns of a sociologist working back and forth over the dangerous no man's land between sociology and theology and trying to draw out the images of transfiguration and deformation which I believe are the bedrock of theological thinking.

As an adolescent I wanted to be a poet or a musician, but I became neither. These addresses are the unwritten poems and music.

Note

1 Cf. George Steiner, 'A Preface to the Hebrew Bible' in *All Passion Spent*, London: Faber, 1996.

The Language of Christianity: Story, Body and Sign

God's Transcendence

In thinking about the language of Christianity, I begin with the most difficult topic of all, because fundamental to everything else, our speaking about God, and then I turn to Story, to Image and what I call Giving the Sign. I suggest we look at Christian faith as a code book for picking up signals of transcendence, and the question is how are we to pick up those signals and interpret the code?

Of course, many people will find this odd. Surely it is all much simpler than that. For 'Golden Rule Christians' their faith is about goodwill, forbearance, caring, sharing and going the extra mile. Yet if that is so its appearance nearly two millennia ago was completely unnecessary. Judaism offers all of that, as does the common wisdom of the ancient world and the common sense of our own Enlightenment. We need only consider the ceremony of Candlemas or the half-forgotten language of the religious paintings in our galleries to see that Christianity is more than a divine sanction for decent behaviour.

The first difficulty with opening up the Christian code and interpreting its signals of transcendence is our assumption of familiarity. We miss the strangeness of taking fragments of bread in our hands as tokens of Christ's broken body, of making the sign of the Cross, and of charging the fragments with his real presence in words and gestures of powerful blessing. Again, it is not immediately obvious how dipping tiny babies in water conveys their journey from darkness to light and death to life. This is thinking with the signs of bread and water. We bless these primal elements to imbue them with heaven and colonize them for divinity. It is a kind of acted miracle, a re-incarnation, whereby words become flesh to make divine love tangible.

And if these signals of transcendence conveyed in images and the making of signs are strange so, too, is the story we tell. First there is a Hebrew story of a captive people transformed into a liberated nation trekking across sea and wilderness to a land of promise. But then there is a Christian translation of that story, also with a passage through water and a sojourn in the wilderness, which turns it into a mass migration of the spirit to build a new Jerusalem here, there and everywhere. The migration converts strangers and aliens into citizens of that heavenly city and by grace it frees the slaves to become the sons and daughters of God. This is the great transition anticipated in the passage through the waters of baptism: from the slavery of sin to the glorious liberty of sons and citizens. So the making of signs, image and story all mirror each other.

And they are all grounded in a language about God. Words like transition, transformation, transfiguration, depend on God's transcendence; what passes through and goes beyond. So, to use such language is not to give information *about* God or deal in testable hypotheses, else faith would be science. We invoke the transforming vision. We can never inspect God but only respond to revealing signs of the resurrection and the life.

Yet there *is* a work of the intelligence here. We say God is one and inclusive. In Him is unity and infinity, fullness and order. Just as our grammar cannot work without the omnipresent verb 'to be' so the language of faith cannot work without the 'I am that I am' or 'I will be what I will be'.

God is the real presence of the transforming vision and the beckoning horizon of the perfect and the good. That presence and that 'perfect in the future' press against the gross resistance of our everyday world. To weave the imprint of faith and its images into the fabric of human culture is to conduct the pressure of incorruption against corruption, immortality against mortality, and the perfect against the ruined. Faith is not a leap in defiance or default of evidence but our co-option by grace into that forward movement of the Spirit against what faith identifies as 'the world' or 'the powers'. We align ourselves with a fresh angle of vision on earth renewed and a city restored. We seek to amend the ruin that has so mysteriously entered our garden.

I have already implied that humankind has two singular privileges which are to inspect and to kneel. The second requires we open the lazy eye of the spirit. We inspect by nature but we kneel and adore by choice. Once we, as creatures in the image of the Creator, freely kneel and adore we enter into the delight of the divine wisdom at play in the company of God. We share His pleasure in all creation and in Yeats' phrase we can no longer tell the dancer from the dance.

The Bible asks: 'To whom then will ye liken God?' In our approach to the Creator Spirit and the Keeper of Being we fall into silence before the unspeakable Name. Yet still we have to walk gingerly on the stepping stones of image and metaphor. If we do not the eloquent empty space in the holy of holies might dissolve into the vacancy which lies outside the house of language.

The stepping stones are acts of naming: Shepherd and Lamb, Father and Son, King of Glory and Prince of Peace, Light and Life and Breath. We evoke and invoke, call on and call out; we 'consider' the lilies of the field and the works of his fingers.

> For I will consider my cat Jeffrey
> For he is the servant of the Living God,
> duly and daily serving Him ...
>
> For he counteracts the powers of darkness by his
> electrical skin and glaring eyes
> For he counteracts the Devil, who is death, by
> bristling about the Life.

These 'considerations' are not science but our contemplation of pure gift and grace abounding.

Redemption's Story

From the vertical frame of transcendence one turns to the horizontal frame of history, or rather story, that is to redemption in time. I choose story over history with some hesitation. Certainly Christianity is historical in its interpretation of happenings in time, with their beginnings, crises and endings, their purposes and their consequences. Yet the Bible provides no ordinary chronological history any more than the gospels offer biography. Christianity is the divine comedy of redemption, restoration and regeneration after our fortunate fall into time, and into division, fragmentation, alienation and degeneration. I say 'fortunate fall' because without the deterioration and the potential of time nothing can acquire value, and because without the possibility of evil good is meaningless.

This is *the* Big Story, constantly repeated in liturgy, of our struggle to recover, to buy back, have the debt cancelled, and enjoy second birth. Liturgy does not argue a Christian case but tells the Big Story in dramatic cycles. And in the condensed drama of the Eucharist it plays out the superimposed episodes of the Passover meal and Passion.

The Big Story has its genesis in a collective trauma or problematic situation obscurely glimpsed rather than clearly grasped. It works itself out in episodes of malignant reversal and benign recovery, through constant frustration of our intermittent search for a better way, and a suction towards crisis. Think of the deceitful and opaque transactions in the garden that precipitated time and deterioration, the fratricide of Cain, and of the liberation of Israel that somehow inaugurated just another act in the spiral of violent genocide as the People of God violently occupied the Promised Land. These are the inner dynamics of history that we can best recount as story. Clearly there is a hell to pay for here, and the redemption will be costly, exacting not less than life itself.

Matthew's gospel, chapter 17, serves this argument very well because after the preaching of a better way in the Sermon on the Mount, and warning signs of frustration, there is a clear premonition of crisis. The chapter begins in a transformation scene, once again on a mountain, where the face of Jesus shines like the sun. This scene recapitulates the story so far, partly by looking back to the earlier epiphanies of the Wise Men and the Baptism, and partly by the appearance of Moses and Elijah, representing the Law and the Prophets of the old dispensation. But exalted retrospect quickly turns into terrifying prospect when Jesus identifies Elijah with John the Baptist and in the persecution of the one and the murder of the other foresees his own persecution and death. The old story is about to happen all over again. The violent tragedy is written into the script, though not as yet played out. It is the price of all the violence and expropriation already enacted from the beginning. As always love must pay the full cost of new life. In which case how can this story become divine comedy rather than just another human tragedy? How can what was acted out at Golgotha become revelation and not mere terror?

It does so by a recapitulation of the old story under the old dispensation which diverges by absorbing violence rather than deploying it. Christianity throws into high relief what has been and will be perpetuated and perpetrated in the taking of Jerusalem by violence and it does so through a radical transposition. The migration of an elect people to a promised land becomes transposed into a universal journey of the human spirit ending in a demonstration at Calvary of the Way of Peace. That does not mean Christians can opt out of the moral ambiguities or the inevitable and necessary transgressions of politics in the City of Man. We are not delivered from the local loyalties of blood in family, or land or nation or the constraints of procreation and survival. The old story in the Old Testament remains relevant. We still live in a world where one nation's liberation is another nation's captivity. In any case, it is not a straight contrast between Jewish and Christian because the Hebrew Scriptures themselves initiate that vision of a better city and judgement on 'the world', above all under the tutelage of experience of exile.

Now let us dramatize the contrasts. There is the promised land and the blood brotherhood of the family and nation on the one side; there is the kingdom of heaven and a universal regeneration of the spirit on the other. The two stories are plotted against each other in the same locations and run in parallel time sequences. We can observe the action replay, in miniature scenes as well as on the cosmic scale, until the two stories diverge and a new testament emerges.

Let me illustrate. Both stories begin with births. Like Moses, Jesus is the secret prince and beloved son who is threatened at birth by the murderous king and saved by flight. Like Moses, Jesus is tried in the wilderness. As Moses ascends the mount to deliver the Law so Jesus ascends the mount to deliver all the promises of grace.

One way to come at the recapitulation and at the divergence is to follow through the female line running parallel to the genealogy of Christ: Eve, Sarah, Miriam, Hannah and Mary, plotted against Adam, Abraham, Moses, David and Jesus. Hannah's song at the unexpected birth of a son becomes the prototype of Mary's Magnificat as she ponders, 'How can these things be seeing I know not a man?'

And that moment of birth by the Spirit really is the point where the two stories begin to diverge. The universal fraternity of sons and daughters born of the Spirit starts its accelerating and strife-torn separation from the genealogy of family tree and elect nation. Whereas Genesis with its twinned figures of Cain and Abel, Jacob and Esau, was focussed on the struggle for group survival and the procreation of generations of the people, the twinned figures of Jesus and John are about a *re*generation in the spirit for all who seek a second birth.

'Who is my brother, mother, sister?' Where now is the temple? Unlike David, when Jesus (the 'son of David') comes to Jerusalem he only seeks to capture it for the Kingdom of God and His righteousness. When his body was mutilated and destroyed by the powers of the old Jerusalem, Jesus rose again to become the bridegroom of the New. In that heavenly city it is not the temple but the resplendent Lamb who stands 'in the midst of her'.

The divergence becomes a dramatic contrast as between the central episodes of the two stories. In the one the migration of a liberated people across the Red Sea to a promised land becomes an occupation of territory which drives the alien beyond its boundaries. In the other there is a migration or regeneration of the spirit in search of a boundless kingdom where all are invited in to sit down at the universal feast. The one who becomes the King of New Jerusalem becomes also the new King of Peace.

In the end there are just two stories: Passover and Exodus, Passion and Resurrection. St Ambrose in his hymn for Easter Eve perfectly catches the way they are synchronized, the one recapitulating the other – and their divergence.

> 'This is the night in which thou, Lord, didst first lead our fathers, the children of Israel, out of Egypt, and make them cross the Red Sea on dry land.'
> This is the night on which Christ burst the bonds of death and rose again victorious.
> 'O blessed night which alone was worthy to witness the hour of his rising.'

That is the story condensed in three sentences. The Preface for Easter Eve gives it in one: 'O blessed sin that merited so great salvation.'

Image of the Body

After the vertical frame of transcendence and the horizontal frame of redemption in time, we come to the Christian image of God. The issue here is what the Bible calls the 'express image and likeness' of God located in the body of Christ. It is through, by and in this embodiment that transcendence is made manifest and the story of redemption in time made possible and worked out. Once we focus on that precise incarnation in 'Emmanuel, God with us', we realize the key question is not just whether we believe in God but what kind of image of God we truly entertain.

We have, once again, to remake Christianity in all its proper strangeness. The phrase 'God was in Christ reconciling the world to himself' is familiar enough but rephrase that as the exposure of divinity in a vulnerable human body, born to die, and you have a measure of the Christian revolution in our idea of God. Christian language is a word made flesh, confined in time and space. The uniqueness of Christianity lies in its combination of humanism and materialism, because humanity and matter are redeemed through the body which is also the bread.

Let us step back for a moment. All the prime dialects of faith intersect and agree when they affirm that God, Jahweh, Allah, Brahma cannot be named, thought or represented. We approach God negatively by enumerating what He is not, because that of which we cannot speak resists and transcends definition. God encompasses us and not the other way round.

Yet these languages of faith have to find tangible expression. In Christianity, according to Aquinas, writing as a philosopher, 'God is not a body' – that is, an existence alongside other existences – since He is a spirit to be worshipped everywhere in spirit and in truth. Yet in his hymn for the Feast of Corpus Christi, Aquinas, writing as a poet, confesses:

> Of the glorious body telling
> O my tongue. Its mystery sing.

This is body language, the cosmos in a grain, love's supreme instrument and means of expression. Christ as lover of our souls is wed to us in his body. And because his body was and is exposed to our handling and mishandling we read in its wounds and brokenness the cost of our rejection and lovelessness.

From womb to tomb, and pang of birth to sting of death, Christ's body is the document in which we recognize our lacerated condition. If in the light of his transfigured face we see what might have been and can be, in the marring of his countenance we see what so often has been and must be. It is in the *face* we see the image of God implanted in us, never totally obliterated, and in the broken image that we take the measure of our fall from grace. The one is an index of love and freedom, the other a measure of enmity and fatality.

Leo Steinberg in his book on the sexuality of Christ as depicted by the Renaissance masters shows how they render the whole story of our salvation, with birth and death, beginning and end, each mirroring the other.[1]

Let me offer two of his miniatures. First, the blood flowing from the wound in the Lord's side does not flow downward following the laws of nature but into the groin. This body language is telling us that from the very beginning when Jesus fulfilled the law in his circumcision until the end when he fulfilled it in his crucifixion, he was wounded for our transgressions and bruised for our iniquities. 'The chastisement of our peace was upon him.' Expressed crudely that is bizarre, but viewed profoundly it placards all the long-term costs arising out of the bottomless pit of iniquity, either through the need to maintain the law and its ritual exactions, or through the suffering and generous grace which alone is able to cancel our transgressions.

The second miniature juxtaposes the infant Christ dependent on his mother's body and drawing sustenance from her breasts, with the resurrected Christ at Emmaus blessing the food and giving the sustenance of his body to the disciples. If we translate this language it tells us that he who depended is the One on whom we may depend. He sustains because he was once sustained and has shared our condition.

The Second Adam bleeds helplessly for the help of Adam's helpless race. And that is part of what it means to say that Christ redeems our loss. The story of redemption must include the worst in human experience so that even our descents into hell and our cries of dereliction – 'My God, why?' – are retrieved, and incorporated in the divine comedy. The victorious scars are taken into God because Christ has no reserve powers of Godhead to stave off the consequences of incarnation.

So, then, the master image of the body of Christ, given and broken on the wheel of history, reverses and revises our understanding of God, showing him not solely or merely the supreme 'Disposer' but as exposed to the miracles of birth, life and death. This exposure of Christ initiates a relation of love and freedom. It embodies a person to person relationship with God into which all humankind is invited and it changes the mood of Christian language from remote command from above to an intimate appeal face to face.

All this is a closed book to science and an open mystery to the imagination. It is notorious that angels with their pure intelligences have no access to what it is to be animated and brought alive by love and freedom. They worship automatically. Though they appreciate the mathematics of creation and admire the 'Master of the tides' and the seasons, angels stay baffled by the enrichment of a God who takes frail flesh and dies. Being immortal they lack humanity to comprehend the phrase 'begotten not made'.

The Christian revolution is summarized in our image of God. Just as the physical temple in old Jerusalem has become the Lamb in the new, so the empty space in the holy of holies, witness to the unspeakable Name, is occupied now by a human form like yours and mine, the body of Christ whose Nature and whose Name is Love.

Giving the Sign

What of the way we give signs of the kingdom, especially the symbolic gestures we make in the Eucharist to offer – and accept – the gift of peace, and to invite all humanity to the feast? Offering peace and enfolding others, neighbour and alien alike, are together at the heart of Christian language and liturgy. Perhaps we could see our Christian language as including a set of hand signals of pacification and inclusion. Hands are raised in different ways to bless and receive persons and food, to absolve transgression, to heal bodies and minds, and to restore breaches of fellowship and of the peace. Hands may be either folded together to secure inward peace or extended open and wide to receive in peace all nations, tribes and tongues.

Peace and inclusion. Let us look first at our gestures of peace making in the Eucharist, before turning to the gesture of inclusion. Of course, peace is always a constant refrain and exchange in our worship, but as we look more closely we uncover the crucial link between peace and the offer of gifts. Peace making is bound up in peace offering, in a triangle of exchange between man and man, and man and God. As we seek peace with God we offer and we present. As the gifts of God are presented by the People of God we, being penitent, receive free pardon and remission of all our sins and are robed in God's righteousness. God's Gift is free, not because grace is costless, but because God in Christ has absorbed the cost of breakage and violence in his own body, suffering sentence of death rather than executing it. That is how God freely pours out life for His People. We receive a 'full, perfect and sufficient' gift through Christ 'who is our peace'.

Of course, we know well enough that such a simple account of pacification in worship is an idealization. Both in the Church and in the world outside there remain the persistent realities of our fall into violence, self-will, disgrace, will-to-power, broken fellowship, averted faces, and peace proclaimed where there is no peace. And, unfortunately, Christian language is of little help in the resolution of conflict, because it moves necessarily between the poles of alienation and reconciliation, loss and retrieval, ex-communication and communication, rather than political compromise and reasoned negotiation.

The reality of our situation is that the Eucharist has been at one and the same time the focus of our division and of our unity, as it was two millennia ago at the very first communion in the upper room. Even then as two hands dipped together in the dish, Judas rose from the table into the night to summon the men of violence. Soon the little peace fellowship confronted the men of violence; and Judas's false kiss of peace became the emblem of all enmity and breakage of trust. We now, for our part, inwardly echo these split levels of unity and division, and as Paul confessed of himself, one part of us seeks grace and light while the other part falls into outer darkness. Most of us are spirits of no fixed abode, roaring and raging unpacified. We know too well that lions only lie down with lambs till they are hungry again. We also know we are only enfolded as lambs by the pure gift of sovereign grace.

What, then, of the most difficult sign of grace: the gesture of inclusion which should complement and complete the gesture of peace? Inclusion and pacification are so difficult because we are by social nature territorial animals, establishing and defending our identity against the stranger within our gates and the alien outside. We reinforce our boundaries because we are all gripped by the necessities of survival of our 'own' people in what we call our native lands. The Bible itself often echoes our social nature in its concern for the multiplication of the seed of Abraham in a promised territory. Israel protects its identity by maintaining boundaries and markers: hence its survival.

It is not that these concerns are wrong. Rather it is that the benevolent generation of identity – knowing who we are and whence we came – is also the potential generation of malevolent difference. Spirals of violence and conflict simply express and reinforce that difference. So Christianity, which in its earliest proclamation ran so counter to violence, and denied exclusive identities, was always bound to be pulled into the dynamic of our social nature and become as divided against itself as we ourselves also are divided against ourselves. Brother is at odds with brother as well as with the alien, so endemic are the divisions wrought by the Fall. Our entrapment is universal.

Faced with such profound resistances no wonder Christian language insists on the unfathomable, necessary depths of sin in our divided selves and our warring identities, and demands from us gestures of peace and inclusion. And it is precisely because we are such strangers to the peaceable kingdom and its righteousness that our entry can never be on the terms of our piety or virtue, our wisdom or riches – or our blood. Rather it is because in the searchlight of the gospel we have been stripped of all pretension beyond the common humanity of God's original creation, and then covered again by the grace and the love poured out in the blood of Christ. The long-term realization of that stripping and covering again should be in the way we seek for others the justice, peace and love we desire for ourselves, whoever, wherever, those others may be.

The most dramatic sign of the universal kingdom which restores the original creation is the common speech recovered in Jerusalem at Pentecost with the tongues of fire. This shared language declares that Christ, the manifestation of God and our Representative Man, has – in the words of Ephesians – broken every partition down of near and far to create an open space where all who seek peace may congregate and freely communicate. In that sign the confusions of the Tower of Babel are cancelled, and the future fall of Babylon, the blood-soaked capital of will-to-power and violence, proclaimed and anticipated. All things are to be made new in a New Jerusalem where the Lamb issues indiscriminate invitations to his marriage supper, including many guests brought in off the highways and byways who never expected to be there.

But not yet, obviously not yet, except in temporary glimpses when a wall or a partition caves in – or when momentarily overheard in music. Gestures remain pointers to an eternal fullness lying there in wait, pressing against time, which includes healing of body and mind because that too belongs to our peace. The Kingdom hasn't come on earth as in heaven and so in a precarious world we still pray the Lord's Prayer. Though we sing of New Jerusalem as our home, and the happy conclusion of our exile, old Jerusalem remains a Babylon where nations and faiths war for survival, liberation or domination. These are (like creation and destruction) mixed fruits of a single stem, the tares and the wheat growing together. We have simply to continue making signs of peace and inclusion to whoever may receive them, rejecting either premature hope or premature despair. Christians have been asked to watch and to wait and if we remember how sleep overcame the disciples in Gethsemane even that may prove too much. Perhaps the faith, the hope and the love are 'all in the waiting'.

Note

1 Leo Steinberg, *The Sexuality of Christ in Renaissance Art and in Modern Oblivion*, Chicago: University of Chicago Press, 1996.

I should note that sections of the above are diffusely indebted to Northrop Frye, *The Great Code*, London: Routledge 1982; I would also point readers to richly complementary (and much more) consideration of these themes in late medieval and early modern times in Sarah Beckwith, *Christ's Body*, London: Routledge 1993 and *Signifying God*, London and Chicago: University of Chicago Press, 2001.

Part I
Christian Alignments in Liturgical Sequence

Banner 1 – The First Day: The Creation of Light

Taken from *The Creation: The Banners of Winchester Cathedral* by Thetis Blacker, Friends of Winchester Cathedral, 2001.

Christian Alignments in Liturgical Sequence

Part I follows the sequence of the liturgical year, beginning with a contrast between the endless rotations of nature and the forward movement of time with its judgement and its promise. The underlying theme is that of disfigurement needing transfiguration, deformation needing reformation and fracture requiring wholeness. Advent inaugurates 'high time' for such visions and revisions. Its 'signs of the times' belong not to the world of mechanism and measurement but to callings for us to undertake a journey in inner space. That journey concludes in the gift of the body of Christ, which cannot be demonstrated by force of reason because the gift of the body (or of grace) is a showing or making manifest. It seeks a free response and initiates a dialogue of love remote from the clash of rival propositions.

The words of Christ confront the settled texts of the Jerusalem scribes. But 'the city' cannot receive the words because the inwardness of grace undermines the external works of the law, because they proclaim a reversal of priorities, putting down the mighty and magnifying the handmaiden, and because they inaugurate a spiritual brotherhood and sisterhood which displace the claims of family and tribe. So the prince of peace has now openly to enter the city offering 'the things that belong to its peace'. In what follows the idiom of violence and treachery confronts the idiom of love shared by friends assembled together around the table. Hell (which follows from our dignity and freedom) is let loose and the lethal costs of evil are presented for payment in full. The resources of love absorb these exactions and re-enter them in the account of good.

The local city then dissolves into the gatherings of friends in every time and place; the temple turns into the universal body of Christ; its barriers and partitions are broken down to create a single open space; the transfigured face of Christ now stands in the holy of holies; the friends of Jesus recognize his resurrection presence among them; they assemble under the Victor's flag to pursue the peaceable warfare of the cross. For that warfare they are granted a common Pentecostal speech overcoming the confusions of Babel and are given a vision of a New Jerusalem 'above', the 'mother of us all' supplanting the blood-soaked reality of Babylon.

Advent I: In the Beginning – Creation and Redemption

The blood of Jesus … speaks better things than the blood of Abel.
Epistle to the Hebrews, chapter 12, verse 24.

This first Sunday in Advent opens the first half of the Church's year in which we accompany step by step the story of redemption. But why begin here? Why not begin at the beginning with the Creation of the World? Why are we *so* concerned about redemption?

Imagine, for a moment, a rather different revised liturgy. There would be a whole season centred around Genesis, chapter 1 which would parallel the season centred on St John, chapter 1. The dramatic announcement, 'In the beginning God created the heavens and the Earth' heralding Creation season would complement the announcement, 'In the beginning was the Word' heralding Redemption Season. The first Sunday of this new season would be called Creation Day and dedicated to the Sun, the Moon and all the Stars. A sacred minister would walk through darkness and total silence to the chancel steps to cry 'Let there be Light'. Then, as slender fingers of light gently suffused throughout the microcosmos of His holy temple, the choir would break into a triumphant, 'The heavens are telling the glory of God and the firmament sheweth his handiwork.' The second Sunday of the Creation season would be the Festival of Earth, Air, Fire and Water. We would say together the *Benedicite omnia opera*: 'O all ye works of the Lord: bless ye the Lord' and read for our lesson 'Who can number the clouds by wisdom? or who can tilt the waterskins of the heavens?'

On the third Sunday in Creation Season, we would celebrate the Festival of All Creatures – or Ecology Sunday as UNESCO might call it. First, there would be a protective litany for the birds of the air, the beasts of the field, and the fishes of the sea, especially that great Leviathan, the endangered Whale. Then there would be a second protective litany for tree and verdure, flower and fern, wheat and vine. A solemn moment of silence would follow in recollection of the destruction of creatures and the decimation of resources. On the fourth Sunday we would gather for the Festival of our Common Humanity, or of the Creation of Man, and we would remember that 'Thou hast made man but a little lower than the angels and crowned him with glory and honour.' And here there would be a second moment of solemn silence as we asked ourselves '*What* is Man?' And we would recollect that the Hebrew word 'Adam' for the first of our kind, simply means Man, and the Hebrew word '*adamah*' means earth or clay: for we are merely dust and to dust we shall return. We would remember death. Perhaps the final Sunday of the Creation Season would be a festival of Reverence for Life, for the contemplation of the infinite variety of species and kinds and orders of being; for the returning mystery of times and seasons, seedtime and harvest; for the mystery of Desire, for the cleaving together of man and woman and for the mysterious emergence of the newly-born of all the sons and daughters of Eve.

A liturgy of this kind does, in fact, correspond to the way many of our contemporaries feel, especially younger people. You can see the evidence by casting an eye over the 'green' shelves in almost any bookshop. New Agers, and not only they, feel protective about the earth and about its resources: they desire to save the whales or save the trees or the biosphere. Their rites are rites of natural harmony following the rotation of Spring and Autumn, Midsummer and Midwinter; their temple is any numinous knoll in Arthur's country or Merlin's land. Such people seek after a wisdom of the body, of the self and the earth, and uncover that wisdom by contemplation and natural spontaneity. Wisdom is their salvation, by putting them in touch with the deeper harmony of themselves and their environment.

But there are difficulties, which are partly indicated by a dispute between my youngest son, Magnus, and his dog, Megan. Out of respect for the brute creation, Magnus gave up meat, but he went on to propose that Megan do the same as a measure of cross-species solidarity. He met with a rather 'brutal', indeed I would say a rather dogged response. Megan is a 'good dog', as doggedness goes, but in her part of creation, though it wouldn't be true to say that 'dog eats dog', dog definitely does eat meat. The point is that Megan *behaves* well, but she does not reflect on the nature and quality of her acts, which is to say she lacks language, and morality and history. Megan is innocent and natural; she is *not* Christian. *We*, however, speak, reflect, know good and evil and have been *ejected* from nature into history. Our liturgy has to be a word, and a good word, that is a moral word, spoken in time, that is in history. We cannot live in the garden of nature doing what comes naturally, unaware of time except for the rotation of the seasons and the phases of the moon. We remember, we anticipate, and our language shows we have reflected, and know good and evil. Of course, we are also part of nature and caught up in its rotation of life and death: genesis is the background to our liturgy; St John presupposes genesis; our creed begins with a God who made the heavens and the earth before commencing the history of redemption. The heavens *do* tell the glory of God. But a liturgy which has regressed from history to nature does not speak truth to our condition, even though it cannot evade the knowledge of death and of misuse and disharmony. It has, at least, to have those two moments in silence.

In a way I have said all I can say, as to why Christian liturgy is set in historical time and tells a story of remembrance and anticipation, good and evil, promise and judgement. But let me conclude with a reflection which is not the diversion it may appear to be.

Nature being neither moral nor historical can be accounted innocent. Being natural requires us to cope with disharmony merely by adjustment and to cope with death merely as an item in the natural rhythm of existence. To partake of such an innocence is to share the life of the garden before we became acquainted with good and evil. But in truth we have been ejected from the garden and cannot regress to innocent ignorance. Nevertheless, we pretend, and that pretence leads us into several kinds of abuse. We abuse the idea of innocence by claiming it means moral goodness tried and true rather than this simple ignorance of good and evil. And then we go on to suppress the reality of evil, and claim it is merely the upshot of circumstances, and can be dealt with by altering those circumstances. Therefore, it requires no forgiveness or redemption. Of course, circumstances and contexts matter a great deal. But when we have monitored and uncovered every circumstance, we are still left with the mystery of iniquity and, therefore, with the necessity of redemption. That lost experience and crippled humanity has to be brought back and restored.

The Christian religion is not based on a response to a local disharmony, or on a small crack just at the edge of the human mirror of the image of God. It is based rather on a fundamental fracture or primal crime in which we are all implicated by being human. The true sign of our condition is one man's hand raised against another, or even one child's hand raised against another, whereby the disfigurement of God's image is confirmed in the face of the murderer and in the face of the murdered. Faith is built around an offence, and its heart is the fracture, a sacrificial death which never need have been in the course of nature but, nevertheless, came about by the determinate wickedness of men. That is why this Advent season leaves aside the cycle of nature and instead aligns itself with human history and why we focus on the coming of the good man into the dangerous city, and on time-to-come understood as promise and judgement, disfigurement and restoration, profound disaster and costly remedy. For 'The blood of Christ speaks better things than the blood of Abel'.

Advent II: High Time

> Now it is high time to awake out of sleep.
>
> St Paul, Epistle to the Romans, chapter 13, verse 11.

> Blessed is he that cometh in the name of the Lord.
>
> St Matthew's Gospel, chapter 21, verse 9.

Advent is about what is approaching and even *now* coming to be. We look forward in hope to the benign visitation of the Wonderful Child; we watch in joy and with foreboding the peaceable arrival of Christ at the gate of the dangerous city; we anxiously anticipate times of reckoning as the Lord comes to his vineyard and holds the stewards to account. So, in this way, and in that, Advent is about expected visitations, longed for, or feared, or both.

My theme is time, expecially that fullness of time in the New Testament which St Paul calls 'high time'. But I want to begin by turning over the very stuff of time, because I suspect that somewhere in time's nature lie surprising clues. There are no answers, of course. Faith has no answers, but it does examine clues and wonderingly surmise.

Even as I speak, I am looking forward, sifting my options for the immediate likely future against an horizon of the remote and more uncertain future. I cast myself, we all cast ourselves, ahead of the moment, trying to shape what will become of us. And even as I have spoken, a tiny portion of the fluid future has already slipped by into the irreversible past. Hope and fear have turned into regret or satisfaction. The reel of time never unwinds backwards, raising the dead, reversing constant deterioration, reversing the births of the living.

This casting ourselves forward in anticipation is something like casting ourselves in an unfinished play. We envisage our role and our character, determining ourselves. The play is made up as we go along by private conversations carried on in our inner space, and by a dialogue with others, and with several scripts, half-sketched by ourselves and by others. These conversations oscillate between the magnetic fields of hope and anxiety. Hope and anxiety are two daughters of time. Without them the needle of consciousness could not even begin to tense and quiver. I hope and I fear, therefore I am. We depend for our very being on the perhaps, the may be and the may be *not*.

But time has another more surprising daughter: caring and loving. All the motions and emotions of love turn on the movement of time and are bound up with hope and anxiety. I once stumbled across an extraordinary line of poetry: 'And is there care in heaven? And is there love?' And it suddenly struck me that where everything is safe and static and guaranteed, then we are literally careless, dying of boredom without ability to choose, to make or to die. It follows that we cherish the precious, that we know care and know love, because time has given us a limited span and an uncertain, open future. It is because we live at the sharp end of a short and uncertain story that we can even recognize the infinitely precious.

The love of the mother looking into the face of her child has much to do with vulnerability and neediness, but has also to do with brevity. The time-bound is the heart-felt and the heart-breaking. Listen and look: the rise and fall of the music, first light and last light, first supper and last supper, the 'dearest freshness' of the first snowdrop and the dark splendour of the last rose. It is these which are infinitely precious and dear, and maybe we sense something more of infinity in the dearness. Perhaps we are, all of us, all of the time, skirting the margins of eternity, touching its secret emblems, reading its silent heraldry, participating in its miraculous sacraments. Perhaps the eternal we cannot even remotely imagine has from the very beginning infiltrated deep into our everyday world.

I said my theme was time, especially the *fullness* of time. When we turn to the New Testament we find it accentuates time, fast-forwards it. It brings time to a head so that we may *wake up* to the infinitely precious – that which if you miss you miss all else, and that which if you find you gain the whole world. The Kingdom of Heaven is 'at hand'. This is the moment before your midnight and your last hour before your dawn. The unanticipated Visitor is already there, in the dissipating darkness, battering at the door of the heart. 'Behold I stand and knock.' You are asleep in your 'chamber of bone', but it is high time you were alive to what you should most truly hope for and what you should most truly fear.

The story of the New Testament enters into our own unfinished stories as a partner, infiltrating those inner conversations with its special urgency. It is the story of stories, illustrating what we have to look forward to, what we may anticipate, and speaking of those things which belong to our peace. And what are those?

Well, we may all anticipate a calling to account. That has to be part of it or nothing makes sense. Reckoning comes, not on some last day in mechanical clock time, but on a last day which has been brought forward to the very edge of the present, into the virtual Now. And that reckoning is very simple. If we have embraced possession or people or things and been ourselves possessed by the love of power, then we flail in frantic emptiness and experience the dissolution of all relationships. But if we open ourselves to the empire of the heart we are heirs to all the gifts of God, pressed down and running over. And beyond that unavoidable reckoning we should, most of all, look forward to and cherish every sign of the advent of the human face of God, in Christ. The heavenly kingdom is *there*, in the child held in the mystery of love's embrace, manifest in the sacred bundle of new life. And the heavenly kingdom is also *there*, as the unarmed man comes with open hands to the gate of the dangerous city, aware of the gathering powers of darkness, but offering those gifts which belong to our peace for whoever is willing to receive them.

Advent III: O Sapientia

I take my first text from the first of the seven – sometimes eight – greater antiphons that quicken the pace of Advent in the last seven days before Christmas, and my second text from the eighth and last. These antiphons frame the singing of the Magnificat at the Evening Office, and are known as the 'Os' because they all begin with 'O'.

The first, 'O Sapientia', invokes the Divine Wisdom, also known by the feminine noun of Sophia:

> O Wisdom, issuing from the mouth of the Most High, playing all over the round earth, sweet and mighty, source of all order: come and teach us the way of prudence.

The last antiphon, addressed to Mary runs:

> O virgin of virgins, how shall this be? …
> Daughters of Jerusalem, why do you marvel at me?

I want to meditate on Sophia and Mary, whom many see as embodying very different, perhaps opposed principles. What these prayers make clear, however, is the intimate relation between Sophia understood as Divine Wisdom or Holy Spirit, and Mary whose womb brought forth the Eternal Word in the form of a baby. The prayers are, of course, mosaics of quotation, the first picking up Proverbs, the second Luke and the Song of Songs. It has been the genius of Christianity creatively to rearrange mosaics of phrases, metaphors and images – which in these particular prayers infiltrate our minds with the mystery of a Divine Wisdom existing to all eternity, and a wisdom manifest in brief time and little space. That is the poetry of our creed: 'and was incarnate by the Holy Ghost of the Virgin Mary'.

What we have in these prayers is sign language, and today we still have restricted access to it, for example, through carols or paintings – that is, through what we sing and what we see. I have in front of me four postcards of paintings by Fra Angelico, Fra Filippo Lippi, Lorenzo Lotto and Titian, each of them depicting the dove of the eternal spirit, Sophia, pouring out divine rays onto the head or womb of Mary, while in two of them the angel presents her with a lily. I suppose the lily is another echo of the Song of Songs such as we find in the line 'In the beauty of the lilies Christ was born across the sea', which reminds us that our greatest hymns (and sermons too) are also mosaics of quotation. Prayers, hymns, sermons, are echo chambers of quotation concerning what is known by heart and inscribed there.

Indeed, that is a central part of how we become Christian in the first place, by absorbing its sign language into our hearts like miniature sacraments. There is nothing in the mind, said Thomas Aquinas, that has not come first through the senses. So our access to God, the unimaginable plenitude of glory, is through signs of the spirit heard with our ears, seen with our eyes, held in our hands, above all our handling of the Word made flesh. That, William Temple said, is the materialism of Christianity, a faith embodied in sound or picture or token, and undergoing endless creative rearrangement such as we find in these four postcards – or in the luminous intimations of the carol:

> Enough for him whom cherubim and seraphim worship night and day,
> A breastful of milk, and a manger full of hay.

At Advent and at Christmas time especially, we should not think of Christianity in terms of how many impossible things we can believe before breakfast. Rather we should open our minds to the way the Christian imagination, from Luke and Matthew to a host of later painters, musicians, hymn-writers, and preachers, has interpreted in sign language the mystery of an eternal God whom no one has seen and who also has been seen, known and handled.

In the Christmas story revelation takes place as the first light of creation pours through the night air near Bethlehem, and the angelic choir sings 'Glory to God in the highest'. The receiving senses are sight and sound. But the key message is delivered through the humblest of tangible signs, 'Ye shall find the babe wrapped in swaddling clothes and lying in a manger.' First light is also new baby. We have arrived at the human sense of touch.

The pre-eminent signatures of the creator–spirit in the Bible are light and air, light through air, air as wind and movement. So in one of these picture postcards the rays of light from the eternal sun pass through air to bring Christ to fruition in what Christian imagination (creatively reworking the Song of Songs) saw as the enclosed garden of Mary.

All these signs speak of the expectation of prophecy, which is why Mary is so often depicted reading a book. In her eyes, which are the organ of her soul, the sacred text speaks of bringing to pass what is written, so that both written and eternal Word are to become manifest in her.[1] The words she reads are, '*Ecce*' – 'Behold a virgin shall conceive and bear a son, and shall call his name Emmanuel, God with us.'

The first letters of the seven greater antiphons arranged backwards in the original Latin form give us the Advent message: '*Ero cras*' or 'Behold I come quickly.' May the written and the eternal Word also become manifest in us.

> O Divine Wisdom,
> O Adonai,
> O root of Jesse,
> O key of David,
> O Dayspring,
> O King of nations.
> O Emmanuel.

In the words of the Evening Office for Christmas itself: 'While all things were in quiet silence, and night was in the midst of her course, thy almighty Word, O Lord, leapt down out of thy royal throne. Alleluia.'

Note

1 Indeed, as the Gospel of St Matthew makes specially clear, faith is quotation realized, and a *New* Testament is the appropriation of quotation for a new context. Again, loss of faith is closely linked to loss of the quotations we have by heart: a sign of dechristianization as notions replace precise recollection.

Advent IV: A Word in Time

> God who at sundry times and divers manners spake *in times past* ... hath in *these last days* spoken unto us by his Son.
>
> Epistle to the Hebrews. Chapter 1, verse 1–2.

> The Lord is at hand.
>
> St Paul's Epistle to the Philippians, Chapter 4, verse 5.

My subject on the last Sunday in Advent is a Word spoken 'in time', at sundry times in the past and in various ways, and finally in 'these last days' by the Word made flesh. I begin with what may seem quite remote: the creations, recreations and redemptions of musical time, and the painted icons or images which speak to us simultaneously with no temporal dimension whatever. Then I turn to the recollections and anticipations of liturgical time, and to the retrospect and prospect of the Christian story.

I once attended a piano recital in Boston given by a young Korean woman. The main work was Beethoven's Sonata in A^b major, Opus 110, which he directed to be played with love and singing. It was a remarkable experience because I wanted to ask, 'How do you, child, not yet twenty years old, know what Beethoven knew and for that matter what Alfred Brendel knows?' As I listened I was taken out of clock time into a different world of perfect timing, dictated not by equal units of seconds and minutes, but by sublime argument under the scrutiny of acute musical intelligence. By total subordination to the musical text the young woman had practised the real presence of Beethoven the creator and in that office or service had acquired a perfect freedom. The 'technical', meaning the calibration of the piano and the disciplined habits which determined the myriads of neurons firing in her body, lay entirely at the disposal of spirit. It was word made flesh and flesh made word, and a kind of redemption of time. But meaning what? After Beethoven himself had played a sonata he was asked what it meant and replied by playing it again. That was as much as to say: I begin and I follow it through to the appropriate end; I initiate that which in the final analysis I accomplish; and between that Alpha and that Omega I traverse the whole alphabet and gamut of experience.

Close by, in a room adjoining the concert hall, was an image of the Virgin and Child by Botticelli. Botticelli, as it happens, believed himself in the last days of the world, or maybe of *his* world, but in taking his time to create this image he worked entirely on a single plane of space and extension. Everything depicted on that plane or surface, spoke to you simultaneously, once you had given it some of your time. The picture was now suspended in its own eternity giving itself back to you in the twinkling of an eye.

Of course, to receive such a gift you had to learn a sign language, otherwise to the unseeing eye it was just a woman in blue with a baby mysteriously raising his fingers towards a bunch of grapes and wheat stalks. But once interpret the signs and the picture showed the Blessed Virgin bearing the fruit of her womb, Jesus, as he blessed the fruit of the earth to make it his body and blood. The Word made flesh was also flesh (or material) made Word. Incarnation and Eucharist, though separated by thirty-three years, had been collapsed into a single frame: the abolition of time.

The drama of the liturgy takes more or less an hour by the clock but it condenses history in a unity of time past, time present and time future. The moving finger of each moment in the here and now remembers and presses forward, accumulating, recapitulating, all our temporal experience. It looks back to recover and redeem our losses by a constant cancellation of our constantly incurred indebtedness. It wipes out the consequences of the Fall and our persistent falling away by holding us up before God, through Christ; it foreshadows a kingdom in waiting in God's good time. This good time has not much to do with shadows creeping across the sundial but rather with a midnight which is simultaneously a dawn. Time is brought forward, collapsed, because 'The Lord is at hand' and the fruit of the womb which is also the fruit of the earth, lies already present on the table as our medicine of immortality. This is the newest hour, time's renewal, the millennial dream made manifest.

Clock wise January 1st 2000 A.D. begins Y2K. You have to be clock wise, otherwise you cannot solve a crime, adjust a computer, or calibrate the stars. But none of that *signifies*: not *us* but *that* is insignificant. January 1st, Y2K, is also the Feast of the Circumcision which can signify everything simultaneously, because it proclaims that the first wound of the law and of a limited lineage is, at one and the same time, the last wound on Golgotha out of which flows a universal grace.

Liturgy is progression realized in seasonal rotation; but what of the Christian story pressing forward to the redemption of time in Christ, to the fullness of time in the heavenly city? Christian story is not history understood as the causal sequence of the things of time but the pressure of callings and hopes on history seeking to remake it in a different image. Think of the divine call to migrate by way of a passage in the wilderness, to discover a freedom and a country, to become a righteous nation under God and under His law, to build up the walls of a better city. Think also of the voice in the desert requiring a journey in time, in space and within your inner space, which puts you in covenant with a God unnameable, unimaginable, whose holiest of holies is empty space and silence.

The New Testament is a radical revision of all that, so much so as to be more revolution that evolution, though the Christmas sequence of nine lessons sounds natural enough. That is the New Testament retrospect read and arranged as Old Testament prophetic prospect. Of course, the wilderness and the solitary place are still there in the New Testament, as well as the migration to a better city, but think what has become of the first chapter of Genesis when recast as the first chapter of John. The creation of the heavens and of the earth and its fruits becomes also the birth of a child, the fruit of the womb. 'Let there be light' becomes the light of men in Christ, which cannot be overwhelmed. In the New Testament the unnameable is given a Name above every name, and in the empty holy of holies there stands a vulnerable but glorified human form. The Word in the desert which broke all the idols in pieces speaks again in 'these last days' as the express image of the Father in the Son: at Bethlehem we find 'the Ancient of Days but two hours old'.

Epiphany: A Showing to Visitors

And the Gentiles shall come to thy light and Kings to the brightness of thy rising.
Isaiah, Chapter 60, Verse 3.

Epiphany means 'manifestation' or 'showing'. What we recollect at Epiphany is one of the most basic gestures of humankind: the showing of the child by the mother to others, to all those who come with good hearts and greetings, with gifts and with adoration. At the beginning of the feasts of Christmastime and Epiphany, we celebrate the fundamental process of emergent life, which is the bringing forth of a child and the cradling. But now we celebrate this second movement in which the mother picks up the child and shows him to benign visitors. Nothing is more familiar and homely in all human experience than this, and nothing more full of grace and truth. The mother invites friends and neighbours, strangers and visitors to come and see; and they in turn present themselves and their gifts.

Painters have recognized the potency of this gesture, especially perhaps those of the early to mid-Renaissance, when there was a unique concentration on the life of Christ and of his mother. Again and again painters turn to 'The Adoration', composing the figure of mother and child, and the worshipful shepherds and kings against a receding landscape of hills and townships. Sometimes the landscape was serene and Arcadian, but occasionally there were touches of menace or signs of the ruination of the old order: a blind light-shunning owl or a dilapidated inn. Very few other gestures could draw the painterly imagination in a comparable way; perhaps only the outstretched arms of the impaled Redeemer and his hand raised in blessing at the Last Supper. All these fundamental gestures were and are acts of offering, gifts of the body, or a word made flesh in humanity and in meat and drink. So behind this showing or this manifestation of the holy child we are to discover the most profound layer of Christian understanding: this is my body.

Of course, all these miraculous icons of the adoration, which inform our imaginations and decorate our Christmas cards come out of the original pictures shaped by the evangelists. The earliest Christians designed a mosaic of phrases, picking up fragmentary anticipations in the Old Testament and re-using them to yield the lineaments of Christ and to signal a dramatic enlargement of human hope. 'The desire of all nations shall come'; 'the people that walked in darkness have seen a great light'; 'the Gentiles shall come to thy light and Kings to the brightness of thy rising.'

And, we now, scanning the visual icons and reading the mosaic of phrases – how should we understand them? How can we unlock the elements of meaning? Let me indicate a shift, a coming-together and a reversal.

There is, as St Paul suggests, a shift from the hidden and secret to the open and revealed, and a shift from the localized to the universal. There is also a *coming together* – of youthful and venerable, of kingly and common, of urbane and homespun, wise and simple. The innocent child faces the urbane magi and the wise adore alongside the simple. And there is above all Christianity's great *reversal*. The true king is the child and the true treasure resides in the mystery of Christ. Everything turns on the Christian paradox:

> Welcome, all wonders in one sight!
> Eternity shut in a span.
> Summer in winter. Day in night.
> Heaven in earth and God in man.
> Great little one! whose all-embracing birth
> Lifts earth to Heaven, stoops Heaven to earth.

But how best to envisage the wise men themselves and their wisdom? I confess I am not quite sure what kind of wisdom the wise men represent. I suppose it is some unstable mixture of mathematical and magical, of astronomy and astrology, even perhaps of prediction and fatality and providence. At any rate they are the Masters and the Knowers, possessed of power and the pleasure of understanding the causes of things. They exhibit the sheer delight of intelligence, deploying powers for evil and for good. So we can see their obeisance before the holy child as placing skill and power and intellect under the supervision of incarnate love. Mastery is mastered by wholeness and holiness, and knowledge harnessed by tender concern. The determinations of astrological calculation are finally arrested 'over the place where the young child lay'.

That at least is part of the meaning. But specially the wise men represent the universal scope of redemption and the extension of hope to all the human race. Christianity is not simply a matter of our individual redemption but a renewal of the whole kind: *our* kind. The ancient Latin hymn runs *Veni Redemptor* Gen*tium*. Come Redeemer of our race. *Gen*tiles are all those who look back to a common parentage and share a common name. So out of this nucleus of a single family there emerges the universal family, and out of the fruitful genealogy of the holy child comes the solidarity of humankind. The light that is dramatically narrowed to this prism issues again as the light of the world.

Here in this homely showing of a child to the visitors, some neighbours and some strangers, some simple and some wise, is initiated an action and a re-action designed in an ever-expanding circle of opened treasures and gift-giving to feed and restore a lost and ruined world. In all the landscape round there may be chaos and fear and menace but at the centre faith has composed this miraculous icon of what it means to adore, to offer the heart's oblation and to discover the express image and likeness of the Eternal Father in the face of the Eternal Son.

After Epiphany: Incubations of Hope

> The people that walked in darkness have seen a great light: they that dwell in the land of the shadow of death, upon them hath the light shined.
>
> Isaiah, chapter 9, verse 2; St Matthew's Gospel, chapter 4, verse 16.

St Matthew's gospel quotes the prophecy of Isaiah. Like all the New Testament writers the author of Matthew framed his understanding of Christ out of the Hebrew scriptures, and Jesus himself must have founded his self-understanding in the same way. Many of the quotations framing the retrospect of Matthew also must have founded the prospect for Jesus. In the two decades of preparation, between work and meditation, as Jesus moved about the region of Galilee, with its contrasting cultures (and the nearby classical city of Sepphoris) this particular scripture must have quickened his imagination. It places the dawning of a new day and the birth of a son and a righteous king precisely in the unconsidered margin where he exercised his trade: the periphery of the periphery of the empire. With his earthly father presumably dead perhaps Jesus also took such clues to explore a relationship of spiritual son to heavenly father and with that the freedom it gave him to begin a universal fraternity in the spirit when the time was ripe and the day had dawned.

But the sacred narrative in the Hebrew Scriptures offers many possibilities and different options, such as Joshua the military leader or Gideon the conqueror of the Midianites. Even the promised son and king in Isaiah offers alternative characteristics, such as Mighty Hero and Prince of Peace. Jesus sees himself foreshadowed in the Prince of Peace rather than the mighty hero, as one whose only triumphal entry will be made on an ass. He identifies his role as Son of Man as well as Son of God.

Who in turn will identify him as he walks incognito by the lake and takes part in the life of the synagogue at Capernaum? The question, 'Whom do you say that I am?' implies no explicit disclosure. 'Is not this the carpenter's son?' they say, or 'Can anything good come out of Nazareth?' 'He was in the world and the world was made by him – and the world knew him not.' 'He came unto his own and his own received him not.' Even at his trial when questioning Pilate asks 'Art thou a king?' he reverts to his favourite self-description, Son of Man. You shall see 'the Son of Man'. The Kingdom of God is made known in, through and by the Son of Man. It is the ancient story of the Prince secretly present in the form of a servant.

So then the long incubations of prophetic hope are realized in the unregarded place in the unexpected way. The light to lighten the Gentiles will shine but only to be extinguished by a sword piercing the heart. The world's light will be arrested at night by the powers of darkness. The sun of righteousness rises with healing in its wings but only by a passage through the valley of the shadow of death. Such scandalous reversals are, says Paul, the unexpected power of God to salvation. It is the warfare of the cross that secures our peace because the foolishness of God is wiser than the wisdom of men.

This scandal of the unexpected begins with the epiphany – or showing – in disregarded Capernaum. It leads immediately to the calling of disciples to form a nucleus of the universal fraternity of all the sons and daughters of God, and then by the making whole of the diseased in mind or body. The fourth chapter of Matthew opens up into the epiphany of the fifth chapter when the kingdom is proclaimed from the mountain top in vistas which offer a new charter of peace. The inhabitants of the kingdom are those hungry for justice and persecuted for the right, those who show mercy, are pure in heart, gentle in spirit, forgiving and forgiven. Such are 'in the light' as their Lord also is 'in the light'. Finally the pattern of the kingdom leads on to the pattern of prayer: they hallow God's name that his kingdom may come on earth as it is in heaven. Thy kingdom come, thy will be done.

This is, of course, not a political kingdom. The Prince of Peace is not 'the Prince' of Machiavelli. It is the germ of a perpetual epiphany whereby Christ is the first-born of many sons and daughters of God who gather in his real presence, by small companies or great, to feast and share at a common table. Light still contends with night, and dawn with darkness. The light still shines in darkness and the darkness 'comprehends it not'. His own do not receive him. But to as many as do receive him he gives power to be reborn as sons and daughters not of the will of the flesh or of the will of man, but of God.

Purification: Biological and Spiritual Birth

Blessed art thou among women.

St Luke's Gospel, chapter 1, verse 28.

On this Feast of the Virgin, I want to meditate on what Mary can mean for us. After all, apart from the Lord's Prayer, these words of salutation in the text are spoken more frequently among Christians than any others. For well over a thousand million Catholic and Orthodox believers the Lord's Prayer and the Hail Mary are twin petitions.

And yet what we find in the biblical accounts is quite fragmentary. More than that, some of the fragments indicate a distance between Christ and his mother. When the Lord is told that Mary and the rest of the family are outside looking for him, he says that he finds his real family in the brotherhood of the Kingdom. When someone in the crowd following the cross blesses the breasts that fed him, he says that blessings belong to those who hear the word of God. So we have incomprehension and distance, a gap between mother and son. It is the kind of gap which usually opens as children begin to locate their own truth and discover an independent self. No finding without breaking.

There is a slightly different source of this distance between Mary and her son. Let me put it this way. There are the claims of the biological family, which are local, and there are the claims of spiritual affinity which can extend to anybody. Humans come to *be* through a crisis in the womb, and a crisis of spiritual calling. So what is rightly claimed for the family 'after the flesh' is countermanded by the claims of spiritual fraternity. You must honour your father and your mother; and you must hear the word of God and do it.

So then, as we observe this separation of mother and son we are drawn to reflect on a shift. It is a movement from physical birth and physical incorporation in a family, to rebirth in experience and acceptance of disciplines in a community of faith. Physical generation, which is inevitable, widens out into the free and open possibility of regeneration, coming alive a second time. Gradually the secure cosmic shell dominated by the seemingly permanent figures of parents, cracks open to reveal nothing but an empty sky, and we are alone with inner promptings. We are on our own with 'the voice of our calling', as well as with falsity and fantasy.

Spiritual maturity and genuine choice require a distance from the mother. We declare our independence of the protecting powers of childhood. Christ too made a declaration of independence, from the time he became totally absorbed on his 'heavenly father's business' in the temple to the time when he drew around himself the brotherhoods and the sisterhoods of the Kingdom. Everything had to be set aside in order to fulfil the will of God 'on earth as it is in heaven'. That is a language of priorities. The challenge of spiritual integrity and the pursuit of wholeness supersedes all other. 'Seek ye first the Kingdom of God ... ' and all these other duties will find their place.

So then, by a great transition, which eventually leads through Jordan and the Wilderness, Christ discovers in himself a novel sonship in communion with the Eternal Spirit. A son of Mary is also the son of God. He was united once to the mother in the womb; he is united for always to the divine Spirit, 'fathering-forth' all things.

But this passage away from the mother, occurring between the breaking of waters in the womb and the uncovering of divine sonship in the waters of Jordan, is only one aspect of what we observe. There is also a return of the mother, visible in Luke's account of the holy birth, and in the narrative of the Passion. The female figure who passed into the background, returns to the foreground. *Stabat Mater*: the mother stands, once again mysteriously present. Alongside the redemptive action of the Son there emerges, in the spiritual history of the Church, the redemptive action of the Mother. By which I mean that both, by singleness of mind and obedience to calling, became means of grace. Both mother and son answered the demanding onset of the spirit with 'Be it unto me according to thy word'.

In this way the Mother has returned to take a place by the Son, standing by him in luminous proximity. She literally stands by her son, and in the tender exchange from the cross, her son seeks to protect his mother. They are united in sorrow, love, and care-fulness. So, in the Christian imagination ever since, Mary stays with her son, and stays present with all her spiritual children, especially at birth and death, when the body emerges and when it dissolves. 'Pray for us sinners now, and at the hour of our death.' The icons of this presence are the triumphant gracious woman, holding up her infant for the world to see, and the sorrowing woman, holding the body of her murdered son across her knees. If these are not emblems of grace and protection where shall we find them?

Nor is Mary with her son only in emblems of protection and care. She stands with and by him in the reversal of the power and riches of the world. Mary continues to sing Magnificat 'in tones surpassing' fierce; 'He hath put down the mighty from their seat'. The hierarchy of proud lords and ladies, and of kings and queens, is overturned by a lowly lady and a humble king.

Of course, over centuries we have shaped the Virgin to our needs and prejudices. The figure of an ancient fertility goddess has been remoulded as sexless maternity. Perfect womanhood has been held up as a pure and passive recipient of active masculinity. Extravagant reverence for the Virgin has gone with extravagant denigration of woman and womanliness. Every kind of tinsel miracle has been foisted on a plaster and vanilla Virgin. No wonder that in the vast modern basilica to our Lady of Guadalupe in Mexico City they have shifted her image sideways from the vertical line of the cross to remind everyone where lies the true axis of our redemption.

In the end, the presence of a mother is not to be set aside. Poetically, imaginatively, our creed turns on *ex Maria Virgine*, which is to say on a woman who stands in her joys and pains as the narrow doorway of Nativity.

When I was at Ephesus in western Turkey, I observed there three traditions as to the identity of God. There was the radical, imageless and militant monotheism of Islam; the earth goddess of Diana, sculpted with a thousand breasts; and Mary. Mary's shrine is secreted in a mountain overlooking the city. Her grotto is sheltered, and out of it comes a small stream credited with healing properties. The figure of the Woman is beneficent and surrounded by nature in all its restorative aspects and powers. As you approach her the quietness intensifies and you light a candle to all she offers and embodies.

It seemed to me at that moment that a faith is revealed in its fundamental gesture. Below in Seljuk I had glimpsed through an archway the fundamental gesture of Islam; prostration in prayer, and recitation in a simple space *devoid of figures*. Up in the mountain the fundamental gesture came now from a human figure: a woman carrying and bearing grace in her *body*. I was – and am – admitted into the presence of grace-full bearing. Ave Maria. Hail Mary, full of grace. Blessed art thou among women. And blessed is the fruit of thy womb, Jesus.

Sexagesima: From Lakeside to City

> Behold a sower went forth to sow his seed.
>
> St Luke's Gospel, chapter 8, verse 5.

A parable such as this reminds us that the gospel of Jesus Christ did not come out of the city. Jesus came from a fertile lake district and when he set his face to go to the city he met his death.

Everything that happens in history is very unlikely, but nothing is more unlikely than that reminiscences of words cast on the lakeside air should be built into the foundations of the cities of Rome and Byzantium, London and Paris, St Petersburg and São Paulo. And why? Because no city could for one day take no thought for the morrow nor could it give all its goods to the poor without panicking the Stock Exchange. As the City of London roundly told William Temple: your faith and our money and power don't mix. There is nothing in the gospel for the merchant as merchant or for the lawyer as lawyer, or for the lover, the warrior, the ruler, the scholar or even the spouse. The most powerful words in history were addressed to us simply as human beings in the language of husbandmen and fishermen. A sower went forth to sow his seed, dropping words into the wind about vine and fig tree, lily and mustard seed, bread and fish, and living water drawn from the well. And these words knock at the door of the human heart to ask just this: do you wake or sleep? are you alive or dead?

Since that time the city has found strategies for coping with the awkward words of Christ, either by polite evasion or by outright rejection. I want now to look at some of these evasions and rejections because we can learn as much about faith from opponents as from defenders.

Take, for example, Lord Melbourne, a highly civilized Prime Minister, who said he was a buttress of the Church because he supported it from outside. One day he warned a Cabinet meeting that things had come to a pretty pass when religion was allowed to invade one's private life. He was right. Christianity is more about mending the inward affections of the heart than it is about the external regulation of behaviour. Another critic, Matthew Parris MP, writing in *The Times*, condemned the Church for what he called the cunning and cruelty of its 'vaguely inspirational talk', especially the two commands of universal love and persistent forgiveness. According to him the command to love your neighbour gives no guidance at all in the practical dilemmas of everyday life and politics. As for forgiveness it is virtually meaningless. I think he is right about love. Love is disconcertingly open-ended and there have even been times when the absence of religious rules and regulation has encouraged a dangerous liberty of conscience. As for forgiveness it surely means holding fast to the humanity of the offender while acknowledging the inhumanity of his offence. All the same, forgiveness certainly has its problems. It can, for example, be interpreted as condonation or exploited a long way past seventy times seven.

Let me quote now a more profound critic. 'What is the meaning of "good"? All that enlarges the sense of power in a man, the will to power, and power itself. What is the meaning of "bad"? Whatever is rooted in weakness. Let the weak and the failures perish: it is for us to see that they perish. What is more harmful than any vice? Active pity for the feeble and the underdog – in short Christianity.' That is the voice of Friedrich Nietzsche proclaiming Christianity better suited to slaves than to their masters. Martin Luther King and Desmond Tutu might well say Amen to that.

So let us concede the case so far. Christianity is justly convicted of love, pity and forgiveness, and of seeking to mend the unruly affections of the heart. That is the seed the sower went forth to sow, and clearly in the secular city it can fall on very stony ground. But there is something worse for us to face. The city does have a case against Christianity, and it is that our faith is unrealistic, sentimental and unwilling to confront moral ambiguity. There are forms of calculation, of self-regard, and of profane energy, of power and even of violence, which are crucial to the maintenance of any serious civilization. And that is why the so-called Christian city turns out not so very different to any other. After all, what moral change occurred when Constantinople became Stamboul except that Jews expelled from Christendom could now find refuge there? Christ spoke of overcoming the world but it looks as if his Church was itself overcome by the world at the very moment of its apparent victory.

How then does the seed of the Word gain good ground in the secular city? Perhaps it happens something like this. First the seed has to be protected in the enclosed garden of the Church. There it is framed by creed and sacred text and nourished by the reverent service of commemoration and hope, recollection and anticipation. At this time, it is our privilege in an unpropitious climate to offer precisely that reverent service. Sometimes the seed lies dormant through long winters of the spirit broken only by rare and scattered blooms like Aidan or Martin or Magnus or Columba. But with the arrival of different times the social seasons alter. Then the seed of the Word plumps and burgeons.

Sometimes that happens within the enclosed garden as with Francis or Hildegard, but quite often the seed blows over the wall to germinate on the margins as with William Blake or George Fox or it is picked up by another religion as part of the competition of faiths. Much growth is underground and it belongs to a secret history of virtue. But occasionally the public Word outcrops in the calculating world of politics. It did so when President Gorbachev acknowledged man does not live by bread alone or when President Clinton reminded Belfast that 'Blessed are the peacemakers'. Because the Word is authoritative for our civilization the rule of violence is seen to be under judgement, even though that rule can never finally be rescinded.

Imagine what it must mean over centuries for the Christian sign language to be imprinted throughout the fabric of a civilization. Think of the difference made – through painting, sculpture, word, music and gesture – where the idiom of violence is juxtaposed with a fraternal supper suffused with the idiom of love. Consider the difference made when the false gods of fatality in the stars or the nature deities of generation and mortality encounter the once-for-all rupture of the Resurrection. 'Whom do you seek in the sepulchre? He is not here. He is risen.' Imagine the humanization of divinity that comes to fruition when the Most High whose name cannot even be spoken is also unveiled at Golgotha and found in that most poignant of scenes: the crucified son cradled in the arms of his sorrowing mother. All these luminous icons of faith cast over the human city the light of another kingdom. And they cluster around this one meaning: ‘This is my body, given for you.’

> See, from his head, his hands, his feet
> Sorrow and love flow mingled down.
> Did e’er such love and sorrow meet
> Or thorns compose so rich a crown?

‘A sower went forth to sow his seed.’ God grant we be good ground.

Quinquagesima: Love and Hell's Dis-ease

If I make my bed in hell behold thou art there.

Psalm 139, verse 8.

Love is the lesson of Quinquagesima but I want to explore love by a strange route. I want to highlight love by exploring darkness and throw Paradise into relief by mapping the territory of hell.

You have to be very careful how you preach about hell because it is much the most tell-tale topic for revealing the rest of what you believe. Its big advantage is sheer accessibility since there is enough hell on earth for us all to have clues about its nature. If there is a problem it lies in the riot of contradictory metaphor. Do we scorch or freeze? Our pictures of hell are in part made up of unpleasant or difficult experience and in part shaped by apocalypses and parables, Dante and medieval painting. But obviously these pictures are not realistic descriptions or useful information. The parable of the rich man and the beggar is to be read as a prompt to conscience not as inside information about the interior arrangements of hell. There is no such place: no lurid lake, no outer darkness or tormenting demons or undying worm. Even St Paul, who spoke of ascending into the seventh heaven in his lifetime, also spoke of a nasty brush with hell: 'Who shall deliver me from the body of this death?'

Many of our private hells have little to do with damnation. We can be chronically anxious but that may or may not feed off our spiritual condition. Human beings are capable of torturing themselves to no purpose whatsoever. Such suffering is hellish but need have no connection with the hell which is absence of love or infinitude of regret.

Often we suppose that the very idea of hell is unworthy of a loving God, and we are right. The celestial torture chamber operated by the omnipotent sadist to keep us in line and to believe in the proper way is a disease of our imagination and morally monstrous. But viewed in another perspective the abolition of hell dishonours humanity as much as its retention seems to dishonour God. If we live in a moral world where deeds and thoughts have consequences then hell must be a constant possibility; and if we are free beings then God cannot deny our right to deny him, to reject grace and refuse Paradise. After all, a God worthy of our worship cannot compel belief nor can he be self-evident. Indeed, I suspect that the denial of God's existence is entirely trivial compared with the rejection of grace. Hell, then, follows from the dignity conferred on human beings by their freedom and from the limitation on God's freedom imposed by his love.

But are we really free? Aren't we creatures of instinct and circumstance? We are. Yet instinct and circumstance only hedge freedom. Aren't we held captive in a bondage of the will and by reason of our nature enclosed in self? We are. Yet this enclosure is not so total as to eliminate a recurrent dream of the good or prevent us being stirred by the touch of grace. There is a sleep of reason but not so profound we cannot be woken or walk upright to life and liberty. The story of Peter released from prison by messengers of grace is an acted parable of the resurrection and the life.

> Long my imprisoned spirit lay
> Fast bound in sin and nature's night;
> Thine eye diffused a quickening ray
> I woke – the dungeon flamed with light.

All our pictures of hell are about the dis-ease of sin and its consequences in time and eternity. Perhaps it is too simple to suggest that we experience this disease when we suffer gnawing regret or pangs of conscience. Those might be hints of salvation. It could be that the worst ravages of sin are so symptomless we do not even suspect their presence. Somebody said of a politician that his leprosy was so perfect it seemed like health. We need not recognize our exile. We can be so wrapped in self that the touch of grace would be too painful to bear. Perhaps we do not desire the nearer presence of God and would be terrified by the demands of sovereign love. Heaven may offer the beatific vision but it is not the highest kind of package holiday, all comforts guaranteed to the divine pleasure seeker.

If hell now begins to sound attractive and heaven demanding then, perhaps, we should pause for a moment to think about the viewpoint of the average sensual man and set it against the dramatic demands presented by the Gospel. Perhaps in our heart of hearts the Gospel only makes sense at the breaking points of life. Most of us, most of the time, want to be morally off-duty, pigeon-fancying or walking the dog, or having a lunchtime sandwich. Salvation and damnation seem overdrawn. We live our lives on a modest scale undisturbed by the possibility of irrecoverable loss.

Yet each of us in our personal lives encounters microclimates of lovelessness, destruction and devastation. Who has never said: Too Late, Too Late or How Long, How Long? The cosy surfaces are misleading. The moral law that the pursuit of self-aggrandizement hollows us out and diminishes us is never abrogated. And sometimes the kingdom of darkness becomes visible so that we catch sight of the face of evil. In Bosnia, Rwanda and Burundi we see it plain; but not only there or other such places of which we know little. Strangely enough such public evil does not require the presence of some dramatically malevolent individual. All that is needed is a downward spiral of ill-will mingled with fear and suspicion which untoward circumstance suddenly sucks into the abyss. Then the masks of ordinary humanity fall away and our faces are possessed by demons. Those who stand as spectators in the half light recoil at the eclipse of reason and truth. It becomes clear the Devil is a liar and the Father of lies as people seek to deny the obvious or justify the unjustifiable. That is the moment we cry out that such hell on earth demands a punishment without remission. As Elie Weisel stood on the ground of Auschwitz fifty years after the event he cried, 'Do not forgive.' On that particular ground the possibility of damnation is a requirement of humanity.

'Father, forgive them for they know not what they do.' I do not believe we are ever in a position to deny the possibility of forgiveness any more than we are in a position to deny the possibility of damnation. And in a mysterious way the cross of

Christ brings together our knowledge of the cost and weight of evil and the countervailing presence of unconditional grace. Christ entered into the dark domain and took on himself its faithlessness, its untruth, its isolation, desertion, condemnation and death. So doing he absorbed the ruthless exactions of evil and entered them in the account of good. The furthest depth of infamy was brought to serve the highest reach of grace.

> Love's redeeming work is done
> Fought the fight, the battle won,
> Vain the stone, the watch, the seal,
> Christ hath burst the gate of hell.

Lent and Ash Wednesday: Fallen Faces and Restored Faces

> The publican … smote on his breast, saying, God be merciful to me a sinner … I tell you, this man went down to his house justified rather than the other.
>
> St Luke's Gospel, chapter 18, verses 13–14.

When Christian ministers preach on the Lord's contrast between sensible Martha and meditative Mary, they often declare a 'sneaking sympathy' for Martha. But when confronted by this contrast between the righteous Pharisee and the humble publican they find nothing whatsoever to say in favour of the Pharisee.

That is not surprising, yet there is a very serious issue here between justification by public works, and justification by a prayer of humble access to God's mercy. The issue has been fought over throughout Christian history; between St Paul and St James, Augustine and Pelagius, Luther and Erasmus, Wesley and the enlightened Christians of the eighteenth century who thought Christianity about ethical wisdom rather than about sinners justified and redeemed. (Of course, once you think about letting the dead bury their dead or becoming a eunuch for the kingdom of heaven's sake or ignoring tomorrow, you can see that the New Testament is *not* just about their kind of ethical wisdom.)

The question raised by the contrast between Publican and Pharisee can be put this way. Just how deeply ingrained is our moral corruption and alienation from God, and how does that bear on our humble abasement before his holiness – and our constant falling away? The question must strike devout Christians every time they receive communion. According to our own confession we have spent the time since last we came doing those things we ought not to have done; failing to love our neighbours as ourselves, engaging maybe in pride, malice, envy and the rest. Nevertheless, we are promised perfect remission provided we seek to amend our lives, which we have just admitted we invariably fail to do. Clearly sin besets us very easily, and though some people criticize the *Book of Common Prayer* for coming back to our 'manifold sins' immediately after communion, realistically it cannot be far off the mark.

Personally I take this realist view (which others call pessimism or cynicism) but there are difficulties both in my position and in the position of the optimist. Realists appear not to expect remission and redemption to make much difference when it comes to amendment of life and a pure heart. Optimists, however, seem to regard the publican as an unhealthy example of low self-esteem, and reduce redemption to moral effort on the part of decent citizens who were not all that bad in the first place.

But surely these alternatives are too simple? Do we perhaps stand on both sides of the paradox or are we maybe just awkwardly ambivalent? Recently a woman, recovered from breast cancer, told me how repeating 'Lord I *am* worthy' helped save her from irrational guilt, and I listened sympathetically, not at all wishing back the guilt-inducing and rule-ridden Catholicism of her childhood. But then I know of another young woman, whose experience of abuse left her with a chronic sense of her own pollution which was only assuaged and her communion made possible, by the Prayer of Humble Access: 'We do not presume to come to this thy table, O merciful Lord, trusting in our own righteousness.'

If we are awkwardly ambivalent, on the one hand about humility and the chronic nature of sin, and on the other about the hopeful pursuit of moral improvement, then that is hardly surprising because we all belong to that world where personal sin is an embarrassing idea, where the talk is all about life-style choices and personal affirmation, and evil is no more than a media spectacle. The Church turns up the volume on self-esteem and affirmation, enablement and empowerment, at the expense of sin, corruption, holy laws, humble access and justification by faith – as though the world might attend to what it already knows.

Not, of course, that there is no theological case for optimism and the works of morality represented by the Pharisee. After all, in the optimistic view we come before a benevolent and rational God created in His image. We are blessed with natural affections inclining our hearts to virtue, and with consciences able to judge between reasonable self-love and considered altruism. And, as members of society, we dare not dispense with such basic ideas as public decency, attention to reputation, and respect for the intrinsic worth of each and every person. Reputation is the key. Just imagine how ridiculous it would be if public life were made up of breast-beating publicans. Each and every one of us has discreetly to let drop that we do indeed pay our tithes and taxes, cherish our ailing relatives and give to good causes.

This is the religion of reasonable people which takes the world on its own terms. It knows we have to make choices and face the consequences. Though we may call it Christianity it is more a kind of liberal Judaism in an enlightened key. Of course, the Pharisee with his well-advertised good works cannot really be recommended, but in some ways he is our man, especially maybe on Stewardship Sunday. What such a faith forgets is the obvious: the million or so piled-up skulls in vast ditches in Rwanda, some even filling the churches.

Such reasonableness and such forgetfulness is not at all the worst reduction of faith on offer. Christianity can even be presented as 'All you need is love'. So infantile a simplification cannot conceive of the destructive and often irreversible consequences of 'the devices and desires of all our hearts'. It knows nothing of the corruption of all our projects, including those like Christianity and Socialism, dedicated to the highest good. It makes nonsense of a faith whose basic story is of the torture and judicial murder of an innocent Son of Man.

How then to recover what Lent and Ash Wednesday mean, with their messages of corruption, mortality, violation and temptation? Maybe, since we so easily fall again and again, we should begin again, and again, with, 'Lord have mercy'. That way we 'open up the crystal fountain whence the healing waters flow'. Why? Because we open ourselves both to humility and exaltation, to keeping our distance and to being accepted, to being judged and being justified. Certainly, we can and must be confident, because in Wesley's great phrase we 'claim the crown through Christ', providing we realize we have not closed the gap between the earthly and the heavenly; or crossed from corruption to resurrection, and wound to health. In ordinary clock time, we think of one thing displacing another and moving on, but in worship time we are simultaneously sinners and justified, creatures with fallen faces and creatures with restored faces – and we arrive only to begin again. When the veil lifts and, with Isaiah, we see the King, the Lord of Hosts, we respond once more, 'Woe is me for I am a man of unclean lips'.

The gap between earthly and heavenly, and between sacramental tokens and the vision, remains because the kingdom in waiting is only prayed for, not realized. We touch with longing but without possession, because we are still journeying. We come, not trusting in our own righteousness but justified by grace and the gift of God. 'Lord, I am not worthy, but speak the word only and I shall be healed.'

The Vigil of Holy Saturday: Violence and Peace

> Put up thy sword into his place: for all they that take the sword shall perish by the sword.
>
> St Matthew's Gospel, chapter 26, verse 52.

> For they know not to do right, said the Lord, who store up violence and robbery in their palaces.
>
> Amos, chapter 3, verse 10.

At the heart of our human situation is the frail fraternity of love gathered around a table. It is vulnerable to treachery, and threatened by violence; to death by violence, and by death itself. All this is written into the Bible from beginning to end. If we take the Gospels alone they begin with a proclamation of peace which is met by an act of state violence as Herod seeks to murder the infant King. They draw to an end with the seizure of the Prince of Peace by men armed with swords and with staves who did to him whatsoever they would. Taking the Bible as a whole it begins with the good creation and the relationship of man and woman. There follows immediately the murder that brands on our forehead the mark of Cain as well as the rational image of God. The Bible ends as the dreadful city of Babylon the Great seeks to destroy the infant Church and is overcome by the Heavenly City of Universal Peace. Thus throughout sacred scripture our fragile fraternity stands poised between love and creation, and violence, destruction, and death. That violence covers every form of malignancy: murder, violation of the person through indignity, rape and abuse, violation of what is proper or precious to another, and violation of the truth. All of that is covered in 'the Law'.

Let us fill in some of the detail of the theme of violence and death. The central figure throughout is Adam, the Man, not just in solitariness but in connectedness with others. We see one man's hand turned against another, not only in the felling of Abel the shepherd by Cain the farmer, but in the enmity between Sarah the mistress and Hagar the servant woman over the succession of their sons, between the domesticated Jacob and Esau the hunter, between Joseph the family favourite and his envious brethren, and between Absalom the rebellious son and his father David.

The turbulence and the division extend far beyond the family. In the story of Babel the peoples in their urge for ascendancy cease to be able to understand one another. In the story of Israel in Egypt a whole people is enslaved and seeks a passage to liberty through the Red Sea pursued by monstrous violence. But then they take the crucial step of controlling and invalidating violence by placing themselves under the Law, and much of the rest of the Bible has to be about their relationship to that Law. Its basis first of all has to be reverence for the Holy and then respect and reciprocity within families and between neighbours. This establishment of Law is the act of Man the rational creature made in the image of God.

So we envisage Man in his astonishing duplicity: stamped in God's rational image, cooperative and creative, and also bearing the mark of Cain, antagonistic and brutish. He is potent with ambiguity, inclining to peace, life and virtue, and declining into violence, sin and death. He incurs the judgement of the flood, and receives the promise of the rainbow and the ark. In a parallel way the City of Man is also potent with ambiguity. Looked at from the viewpoint of monarchs Jerusalem is the city of the Great King whose walls protect peace and prosperity. But in the eyes of Amos the mountain herdsman the city is the site of iniquity. 'Can two walk together, except they be agreed? ... they know not to do right, said the Lord, who store up violence and robbery in their palaces.' So 'the songs of the temple shall become howlings ... and there shall be many dead bodies in every place; and they shall cast them out in silence'. Mysteriously Amos then acknowledges the dynamism of evil by saying, 'Shall there be evil in the city and the Lord hath not done it'.

In the judgement of Amos, then, the lively harmony of human relationships has succumbed to a deathly silence. Yet the judgement is not final because the prophetic vision also includes everyone sitting under the fig tree, the weapons of violence turned into pruning hooks, and the dry bones animated by the Creator Spirit. Such is the ancient dispensation of human affairs which in one way remains with us to this day: death and violence with vengeance to the third and fourth generation, and love and creation presiding over equity and justice. Nevertheless, there is always a profound downward spiral which holds us fast in prison. Both Man and his City are corrupted so that we are estranged from ourselves and aliens to the Commonwealth.

It is the Christian faith that this sombre condition of city and self is encountered by the advent, presence and passion of Christ. With respect to the city a seed is sown at its heart dramatizing the death of the innocent at the hands of the corrupt. A judgement is placarded concerning the presence of injustice in the city. The sign of blood sunk into its very foundation stones is met by a sign of blood shed in life-giving love. That means that above the local city of man, with its potential for death and violence and death by violence, there rises up a vision of the city of God, founded in peace. In the midst of her flow life-giving streams for the healing of the nations, and there are sounds of music and feasting. In that city music quells chaos and the glorious body of the Lamb that was slain takes the place of the temple. (But as for the earthly city below, that remains wrapped in, 'the old miasmal mists'. She can rise no further than intermittent enlightenment because when it comes to redemption the cry of the city is always 'Not yet' and 'How Long?' Look at the state of Jerusalem now.)

With respect to the self there has first of all to be the word of justice and reproof to establish the truth. Should violence be done to truth, justice itself cannot be done. We remain trapped in the cycle of moral debt. But once establish truth, then faith and trust ensure all our indebtedness is cancelled by the free gift of God manifest in Christ. The law of sin and death is abrogated and the gate of heaven thrown open for all who desire to walk through.

In all these mighty transactions the old covenant is not destroyed but fulfilled. There is a great accumulation of signs without the cancellation of any. The goodness of God's creation is affirmed because that is the first and primordial sign of life. Then all the other signs of life are summoned up to confront every sign of death and despair. The image of God in the rational soul of Adam not the murderous mark of Cain; the promise of ark and rainbow not the destruction of the flood; the crossing of the sea from captivity to liberty not the horses and chariots of destruction; the sight of the promised land not death in the desert; the breath of life not the valley of the dry bones; the reversal of Babel in the birth of a universal speech; and in the early morning of the third day the presence of the Lord in the garden of resurrection not the lonely death on the desolate hill. This is the New Adam, the New Covenant, the New Creation.

Resurrection: Singing and the Kingdom

How that Christ died for our sins according to the Scriptures; and that he was buried, and that he rose again the third day according to the Scriptures.
St Paul's First Epistle to the Corinthians, chapter 15, verses 3 and 4.

This affirmation of the resurrection hope by Paul in his first Letter to the Corinthians tells us of the faith of the Church almost in the immediate wake of the actual events. Paul was then as close to the Cross and the Resurrection as we are to the mid-seventies. He knows the actual participants over many years, including James, the brother of Jesus. Indeed, he reports an appearance of Jesus to James of which we have no other record. So from Paul, as indeed from the rest of the New Testament, we know beyond any shadow of doubt what the earliest Christian communities proclaimed. It was the Cross, the Resurrection, and the New Creation in which all the sons and daughters of Adam are brought through Christ into loving relation with God in His heavenly Kingdom. 'Thy Kingdom come.'

This proclamation is woven without seam throughout, and that can be a bit disconcerting because we today gather under the sign of the cross to share in the sacred meal of His body and blood for a variety of reasons. I mean that many of us in all honesty make of our Christianity what we can and give it our vote hoping for the best. Maybe we think of Christ as an early pioneer of social reform or as the Galilean poet of love and good neighbourliness, or as an example of self-giving. We respond to the idea that His spirit is with us to bring us to a rebirth as children of the loving Father. As for Golgotha and the Resurrection, the former is the familiar tragedy of the good man entrapped by evil; the latter is more problematic – perhaps a mysterious metaphor of the recovery of the spirit after desolation or even an analogue of the return of Spring after the dark depths of Winter.

That indeed would be a workable faith, except that its centre of gravity would be differently placed from this proclamation of the earliest church. With such a focus, parts of the New Testament text would become blurred and even unintelligible. By a perfectly understandable instinct we would substitute Paul's great hymn to love at the commital of our loved ones for Paul's equally great hymn to the Resurrection. Yet for Paul, John too, for that matter, love and resurrection were woven in a seamless robe of praise. Love turned on Cross, Resurrection and New Creation, just as Cross, Resurrection and New Creation turned on love. In almost the same breath Paul declares 'the greatest of these is love' and 'but now is Christ risen from the dead and become the first fruits of them that sleep'.

At this point the argument has to move back a step, and if you will forgive me in my coward's castle, I shall risk disagreements. Many of us think of Christianity as an extension of Judaism and regard all religions as witnessing, in varied terms, to a common truth. Well, yes and no. If our stress is on the moral teaching of the New Testament, then there is parallel teaching in other faiths and in the noblest of classical authors, for example, Cicero or Marcus Aurelius. But in that case the New

Testament is really dispensable. If, however, we hold to the New Testament's own centre of gravity in Cross, Resurrection and New Creation, then there is profound divergence as well as profound convergence.

As for Judaism, the earliest Christians were, of course, saturated in the Hebrew Scripture and saw their faith as its fulfilment. That is the point of the repeated phrase 'according to the Scriptures'. Jesus in his many years of meditation in Galilee completely absorbed the meaning of the Son of Man in Daniel and of the Suffering Servant in Isaiah. His followers, reading the Hebrew Scripture in the light of the resurrection, saw Noah, Moses and Daniel as anticipations of it; Noah entombed in the ark until the water subsided and the dove descended; Moses crossing the deadly sea from slavery under an alien law to glorious liberty; Daniel sealed in the lions' den till set free by kingly power. But the Jews mostly read otherwise and they still do. The Hebrew Scripture only became an Old Testament in a Christian retrospect. For that matter, you can see from the Hebrew Scripture, for example, Isaiah, chapter 38, verses 18 and 19, that the earliest faith of the Jews saw little hope beyond death – a fact which incidentally helps rebut the claim that religious faith arises mainly from our fear of death.

Let me, for a moment, interpose a warning from John Ruskin about what may follow should we recoil from the resurrection and try instead to ground faith in general principles of hopefulness or intimations of Spring. He says that as we lose hold of the resurrection not only does the unique music of Christianity in word or instrument fall silent but so, too, does the old Orphic song with its half hope of the return of Eurydice or the song which celebrates the brief and happy interval of halcyon days. Deny the human wishes summed up in 'Thy kingdom come' and there shall be no more singing.

I am not a person much inclined to 'believe half a dozen impossible things before breakfast' or likely to be brave in the face of death. Yet still I ask, how shall we today understand the unequivocal proclamation of the first Christians and of the New Testament? How may we enter into the centrality of those brief weeks between the moment when Jesus and his friends sang a hymn together and walked out into the night of Gethsemane and the moment when those followers toiled all night on Galilee and saw the Lord on the shore in the dazzling light of morning?

We can dismiss the idea that the disciples lied or were the victims of hysterical delusion. People do not base their lives on lies nor do hoaxers or fabulists or hysterics write such narratives as these, including their inconsistencies. Everything written from the earliest epistles of Paul to the luminous epilogue of John's Gospel in chapter 21, testifies to the conviction which revivified the hopeless and scattered company of the followers of Jesus: 'In that he died, he died unto sin once. In that he liveth, he liveth unto God. Death hath no more dominion over him.'

We approach these stories at the heart of faith to find their meaning for us. We know they are not scientific demonstrations of bodily resuscitation. Paul warns us of this and such an idea would turn resurrection into a kind of bizarre experiment offering proof to Caiaphas or Pilate or any dispassionate observer. No, they belong to quite another level of experience. Everything depends on whether you believe the universe is reducible downwards to nothing but covering laws operating in closed circuitry or *gives rise* to emergent properties opening on to the human, the unique and the unrepeatable.

Human story, human creation in painting and music, image and sound, together with the 'markings' on the human face, are all of them unique and unrepeatable. What we encounter with Mary Magdalene in the garden of the resurrection or with the disciples on the Galilean lake or walking beside the Stranger towards evening, is story, new creation and a meeting face to face in which we know even as we are known. The markings are not always immediately recognizable, signifying difference as well as identity, so the moment of love's revelation may wait for the familiar greeting or the gesture of blessing. In any case, the moment of vision is not an opportunity to test tangibility, as you might stretch out your hand to touch the picture or measure the sound waves while you hear the music. New creation, like love, is pure annunciation, as when Peter cried out in the boat – seeing the figure by the shore – 'It is the Lord'. Hymns of love and hymns of resurrection are the same hymn. The trumpet sounds and the dead are raised. As the women came early in the morning through the half-light to find the tomb and to do what has always been done for the dead, they encounter a question and an announcement. 'Whom do you seek in the sepulchre?' 'He is not here.' 'He is risen.' Alleluia.

Easter: The Living Vine

Come and dine.

St John's Gospel, chapter 21, verse 12.

The Jesus who came to his followers and friends in the gospel accounts of his risen presence was both strange and familiar. In the final story from St John he is a solitary figure walking by the lakeside in the very early morning whom the disciples do not recognize. In the chapter immediately before, it is again early morning, and he stands anonymously in the garden. Mary does not know who he is and supposes him to be the gardener. In St Luke's Gospel he is a mysterious third man who joins two others as they walk to Emmaus. Their hearts begin 'to burn within them' but they still do not know it is the Lord.

This is the way Christ visited his friends, in a form which does not immediately reveal who he is. Until, that is, they recognize his sign, his signature, the personal markings which declare who it is they have encountered.

Thomas saw those markings in the wounds of Christ, and said, 'My Lord.' Mary heard herself intimately addressed by name, and said, 'Rabboni, Master.' The two on their way to Emmaus saw hands that broke bread and blessed and offered it, and knew then who had been speaking with them through all the heat of the day. Their guest was their host. They had entertained the Lord unawares.

As for the disciples fishing on the lake they suddenly found their nets full of fish. They exchanged frustration and emptiness for overwhelming bounty. And they knew Him in His invitation: 'Come and dine.' He gave them bread and fish for breakfast. Very strangely they did not dare to ask, 'Who are you?' for then they *knew* (so says the Gospel) that it was the Lord.

These meetings with Christ were not, of course, demonstrations. The risen Christ was not demonstrated publicly to the world. If he had been we would have some very strange and even perverse accounts of how He showed Himself to Caiaphas or to Pilate. There were no reproducible proofs. What happened was – and is – the encounter of friends and the recognition of a real presence, known and loved, knowing and loving.

Above all, these encounters are continuous with what is already known, and with signs already understood and experienced. The marvellous transition from emptiness to bounty, from no catch at all to fishes one hundred and fifty and three, looks back to the first miraculous catch described by St Luke in the fifth chapter of his Gospel. The breakfast of bread and fish by the lake looks back to the great lakeshore feast when multitudes sat down in companies to eat five loaves and two fishes. The evening meal at Emmaus looks back to the last supper and to every blessing received in all the suppers of a lifetime. These are eucharistic signs which speak of the presence of the Lord and the Kingdom of Heaven come amongst us. These moments of blessing, offering, sharing and a real presence *are* the kingdom of heaven. 'I say unto you I will not drink henceforth of the fruit of the vine until I drink it new with you in my Father's kingdom.' The friends of Jesus by the lake or anywhere in the whole world are drinking wine anew in the Father's realm; and they are renewing everything that once seemed lost or waste or fragmented or wounded unto death or broken. They are making all things new from the fragment to the cosmos. The broken bread, the broken body, the lost life, is here re-collected, multiplied and renewed as food for all the children of men. 'So they did sit and eat.'

These signs and signatures of Christ are not immaterial, ghostly things, insubstantial wraiths. They are truly flesh and blood. The form of the material is the manifestation of the spirit. Spirit does not wander about on its own without lodging, but is incarnate and tangible here and now in the body, or in some fish, some bread, some wine, or whatever sustains and gives us life.

Nor is spirit somewhere other than here or confined to a special sacred space or a bible time. So when we read the Song of Songs and place its marvellous secular promise next to the encounter by the lake we are not confused or mixing unlikes or imposing an alien sacred meaning on ordinary human love. Nor are we falsely muddling up the renewal of Christ's presence with the renewal of the earth. We are saying rather that every intimation of renewal, whether it is the new fire of resurrection or the new life of spring can be read as emblematic of the Kingdom. There is no incongruity in saying first, 'Rise up my love, my fair one, and come away, for lo the winter is over and gone', and then saying, 'Rise heart, thy lord is risen, Sing His praise without delays'. He takes us by the hand both as true lover and as most sweet Lord.

Christopher Smart in his poem for Easter Day invokes all the signs of life we may encounter and all the signatures of divinity. He invokes the flowers on the altar because our winter is indeed over and gone. He invokes the singing of choirs and the ground bass of the organ because what should God's people do in the temple except rejoice and what should they do as they enter New Jerusalem except sing? But above all he invokes the victor's flag: the golden sign of the cross streaming out from every spire and steeple. That uplifted royal standard proclaims as it did on ancient fields of battle and in the earliest church that *this* is the precise place and *this* the exact moment when the tide of conflict between good and evil turned decisively.

It is a sign of death too, of course, as well as a sign of life. It means defeat and frustration; it means wounding, loss and waste as well as renewal, recovery and victory, because life and death contend and go on contending down to the very core. One moment we are confronted by closure as we sense ourselves running down, defaced, reduced, just a used-up biological specimen ready for the heap; the next moment we encounter emblems of a different kingdom infiltrating our world with renewal and with promise.

We stand, just now, almost halfway through the season of renewal and promise, between the first announcement, 'He is not here. He is risen', and the final announcement, 'Ye men of Galilee why stand ye here gazing up into heaven?' But where we are in that sense matters less than the promise that 'This same Jesus' comes again, and again, 'till the ending of the world'.

Rise up, my love, my fair one, and come away.
Rise, heart; thy Lord is risen. Sing His praise

Without delays.
Who takes thee by the hand, that thou likewise
With Him mays't rise;
That, as His death calcines thee to dust,
His life may make thee gold, and much more, just.

Easter: The New Name

> To him that overcometh will I give to eat of the hidden manna, and will give him a white stone, and in the stone a new name written which no man knoweth saving he that receiveth it.
>
> Revelation of St John, chapter 2, verse 17.

The Book of Revelation is our greatest store of fantastic metaphor for dealing with cosmic crisis and spiritual war, notwithstanding *Gormenghast*, *The Twilight of the Gods* and *Star Trek*. To some it is repellent, to others profound; arguably it is both. Luther dismissed it till he discovered the Pope might fit the role of AntiChrist. For Nietzsche it represented the resentful imaginings of the impotent. Yet Savonarola acted on it in Florence when he proclaimed King Jesus, and so did the Fifth Monarchy Men in revolutionary England. The Battle Hymn of the Republic drew on it for its 'terrible swift sword' and with just a different twist of history one could even imagine a revolutionary hymn:

> The People's flag is deepest red,
> Are you washed in the blood of the Lamb?

The theme of Revelation is judgement and renovation: 'Behold I come quickly'; 'Behold I make all things new.' It is a tale of the *one* city of God on earth in which the King of Heaven has triumphed over every blood-soaked oppressor. It anticipates the time when the pure in heart have taken over, which history suggests is always an equivocal prospect. It took all Augustine's marvellous intelligence to restore the two cities, one of God, one of Man. With its bottomless pit Revelation is unforgiving, tolerating no neutrals or shades of grey in 'The Lamb's war', yet it is also tender. Remember such phrases as 'Hurt not the earth' beloved of Greenpeace, and 'The leaves of the tree were for the healing of the nations' beloved of peace-makers. On a monument on Boston Common to the discovery of the healing properties of ether I found the tender words, 'Neither shall there be any more pain'.

Everybody fears the ordinary calendar with its ominous prospect of time without meaning, purpose or end. So what Revelation envisages is a liturgical calendar of hope which points forward. We all of us fear chaos, violence and arbitary power, and anticipate what H.G. Wells called 'Mind at the End of its Tether'. By contrast Revelation exults with D.H. Lawrence in declaring, 'Look, we have come through'. It proclaims there is consummation as well as frustration. In Revelation the molten wax of nightmare absurdity is semi-stabilized in a story line we can grasp and hold on to. It isn't science fiction but faith fiction that lends faith wings to soar above the night.

Some suggest Revelation is an ancient liturgy born of distress and persecution. If so it resembles all liturgy in its repetition, invocation, benediction and malediction, in its powerful imagery and imagery of power, and in the way it invites us on a kind of spiritual journey with icons and gestures for markers. St John is taken up on a journey in the Spirit and rather like Dante he is led by spirit guides – and voices. He also ingests the Word. Though it is the Lamb who opens the seals it is the four helpful beasts who invite him to 'Come and see', and they are the four evangelists, each with his own icon or marker: the Lion of St Mark, the Calf of St Luke, the Man-Angel of St Matthew and the eagle of St John. And if the four beasts have their signs so the four horses of the apocalypse have their colour-coding: white for triumph, black for famine, red for war, and paleness drained of colour for death. The primary colours are the red and the white because our 'black souls' have been dyed white in the blood of the Lamb. This is quite a liturgy.

Supposing we look now at just one tiny segment of Revelation about the address of the Spirit to the Church in Pergamos. We need to locate it in what we could call Act I of the liturgical drama which runs from chapters 1 to 3. This is a sequence of addresses to all seven churches in Asia Minor which follow a clear pattern of commendation, chastening and promise. However, this sequence is preceded by a scene setter – beginning with what I shall call the Great Benediction and then the Presentation of the Icon of our Saviour.

The Great Benediction says:

> Grace be unto you, and peace from him which is, and which was and which is to come … and from Jesus Christ, who is the faithful witness and the first begotten of the dead, and the prince of the kings of the earth. Unto him that loved us and washed us from our sins in his own blood, and hath made us kings and priests unto God and his Father: to him be glory and dominion for ever and ever. Amen.

This benediction also hints at malediction because it overturns the oppressive order of the kings of the earth in favour of the servants of God who are each and all made kings and priests 'unto God'. It looks forward to the time when all the earth is a temple because the kingdom really comes.

Next, we have raised up before our imaginations the icon of one 'like to the Son of Man' who was dead, but lives and reigns 'King of kings and Lord of lords'. His hair is white as wool and his eyes a flame. He is 'clothed with a garment down to the foot and girt about the paps with a golden girdle'.

We come now to that pattern of commendation, chastening and promise. Initially the Spirit declares to each of the seven churches in turn, 'I know your works'.

> To Thyatira the Spirit says: I know your works, your charity and service, your faith and patience.
> To Smyrna: I know your tribulation and poverty.
> To Philadelphia: I know you have not denied my name.

But then to each church the Spirit warns, 'I have a few things against thee.'

> To Ephesus: because you have left your first love.
> To Pergamos: because you have entertained division.
> To Laodicea: because you are lukewarm, and neither cold nor hot.

But, after this chastening, there is much good in store for the faithful who overcome. Out of a hard shell comes a sweet kernel.

> To Ephesus: to him that overcomes … I will give to eat of the tree of life which is in the midst of the Paradise of God.
> To Thyatira: to him that overcomes … I will give the morning star.
> To Sardis: to him that overcomes a name in the book of life.

This is not the end because there are yet more mysterious gifts than these offered to Pergamos: 'to him that overcomes will I give to eat of the hidden manna and will give him a white stone and on the stone written … a new name which no man knoweth saving he that receives it.'

The clues to the mysterious gifts partly lie back in Exodus where the wayward people in the wilderness of Sin find their daily food provided, but they also lie in what the Spirit says to Laodicea and Philadelphia.

To Laodicea the Spirit says: 'Behold I stand at the door and knock; if any man hear my voice and open the door, I will come in to him, and will sup with him, and he with me.'

To Philadelphia He says: 'Him that overcomes will I make a pillar in the temple of my God' … and 'I will write upon him the name of the city of my God which is new Jerusalem … and I will write upon him my new name.'

What then could be this supper of hidden manna entering with the Stranger knocking on our door or battering on the heart? It is our bread for today and our spiritual sustenance, which is the redeeming presence made known to us in the blessing, breaking and sharing of bread. What then could be this new name conferring citizenship in the new Jerusalem? It is what is offered in the new birth of all the daughters and sons of God. It is something uniquely theirs in the economy of paradise which no one can donate or take away because it is given to them and them alone under the authority of sovereign grace. It is to become a living stone in the wide temple of an earth renewed. 'He that hath an ear to hear, let him hear what the Spirit saith unto the churches.'

Pentecostal Spirit and the Water of Baptism

> Except a man be born again [of water and the Spirit] he cannot see the Kingdom of God.
>
> St John's Gospel, chapter 3, verses 3 and 5.

If you take the version of this text in verse 3 you think simply of evangelical conversion and 'born-again' Christians, but if you take the version in verse 5 about a new birth by water and the spirit you think also of baptism and Pentecost. The range of reference expands dramatically and a host of images crowd the mind such as Christ incarnate by the Holy Spirit rather than the will of the flesh, and Christ standing at his baptism in the water of Jordan while the dove of the Spirit descends. Other images are the descent of the Spirit in tongues of fire and a universal speech, and Christ breathing the Spirit upon the disciples after the resurrection.

We need some 'joined-up thinking' here because it is very easy to file evangelical second birth and baptism and Pentecost in separate compartments. Perhaps one reason for that is that baptism comes at the beginning of the Gospel, Pentecost at the end and second birth vaguely in the middle. But in the Gospel the end is already present at the beginning so that Pentecost is manifest in the baptism of Christ; and the second birth of all believers 'in Christ' was prefigured by his birth by the Holy Spirit. The contrast throughout (verse 6) is between what is of the flesh and what is of the spirit; and it runs right back to the creation of the world itself, and of man, when the dove moved on the face of the waters and animated humanity so that we became living souls. If the end is in the beginning so, too, that beginning is at the end when in Revelation 'the spirit and the bride say "Come"' with the arrival of the spiritual Jerusalem. In sacred story Pentecost is perpetually present as animation, as aspiration and inspiration, or as life and breath.

Supposing we look separately at Pentecost and then at baptism before bringing them together again. There is first a mysterious closure where Christ is parted from his disciples and then a mysterious opening again as the New Israel, the universal Church, is created by a universal commission and the gift of a universal speech. So, what is happening in that upper room to empower the disciples to go out and preach the Gospel to every creature? It is the emergence of a fraternity released from the ties of family and nation to be global citizens of the spiritual Jerusalem. By the flesh they have been born into the old Israel, with the old Jerusalem as its capital, but this now dies within them as they are born again into the new capital of the kingdom of peace and love. Those who had been only recently local men of Galilee gazing bemused into heaven are now energized to move and create a movement across every man-made frontier. The movement of the spirit sets them on the move by converting them into a pilgrim people en route.

The word for spirit is *dunamis*–dynamism, and the Pentecost present in Creation is now a global dynamic. A parallel word is mission, whose root meaning is to send or be sent. We are talking then about the universal mission recurrent again and again in the sacred story and in Christian history. It is not just an event of biblical times, and at this very moment the most dynamic movement in Christianity is Pentecostalism, to which my wife and I gave 15 years of study. Of course, like every outpouring of the spirit it is ambiguous and follows a curve of fiery expansion and cooling off, but Pentecostals, like John Wesley, take the world as their parish. They are a pilgrim people in the spirit and simultaneously part of today's great trek from the countryside to the megacity. The spiritual transition in which they are born again parallels the physical and social transition.

Let me for a moment expand the comparisons. There were men and women assembled from many countries at Jerusalem and a starburst of fire sent sparks flying all over the then known world of the Roman Empire. So, too, in Los Angeles nearly a century ago (1906) when the Pentecostal revival began, men and women had come together from the ends of the earth until a starburst sent sparks all over our modern globe.

Those 'Pentecostals' in Los Angeles who felt themselves sent in this extraordinary way were loosed from their local ties of family and nation just as were the men of Galilee. All of them, in 36 and in 1906 – we are talking of similar transitions – broke with the genealogy of the local past to create a genealogy of the universal future. What at the beginning in the New Testament had been a circumcision of the flesh to signify membership in a physical Israel became a circumcision of the heart to signify membership in a New Israel of the spirit, present everywhere.

What then of baptism and how is that also Pentecost? Baptism is about a transition in which we pass through water from earthly membership in the natural community to be grafted into the spiritual fraternity of a people whose citizenship is in heaven. It is, so to speak, the certificate of dual citizenship. The Old Adam is a creature circumscribed by fleshly attachments whereas the New Adam is filled with a Creator Spirit to cooperate in making all things new.

I mentioned 'dual citizenship' because in practice we are all people of a local history and an historic place, cherishing natural attachments and the precious genealogy of our family and nation. That is one reason why our baptisms are mostly not total immersions of adults in seas and rivers, as they might be in Jamaica or Ghana, but gentle christenings to indicate and anticipate the claims of the spirit, and of the universal community of the spirit. Our second births are by quiet maturations not turbulent deliveries, and our Christian names appear more as the names by which we happen to be called rather than the sign of our calling. Nevertheless, standing behind all these homely and local ceremonies of purification, acceptance and inclusion, is Jesus immersed in the waters of Jordan to receive the name of 'Beloved Son' as the dove descends; his original birth by the Holy Spirit now become the confirmation of his calling.

So, then, just as there is a common feast of the water and the spirit, all the great feasts of the universal Church are linked together. Lancelot Andrewes, bishop of Winchester nearly four centuries ago, illustrates that in his Private Prayers, joining Pentecost to Baptism, Advent and Creation. For him the spirit moved on the face of the primeval waters, in the prophets and in the Word made flesh. It lighted on

Christ at his baptism and on the disciples after the Resurrection and on all inspired and enlightened by gifts of love, joy and peace.

He prayed:

We would thankfully commemorate,
  in the Old Testament.
Thy moving upon the face of the waters,
Thy sending forth into all things living,
Thy inspiration of man,
Thy descent upon the Prophets.

  Thy Visible Advent

As a shadow;
  Thy coming upon and overshadowing
    the Blessed Virgin
    at the Conception of Christ.

As a dove;
  Thy coming in the shape of a dove
    upon Christ in Baptism.

As breath;
  Thy coming upon the Apostles
    in the breath of Christ
    after the Resurrection.

As fiery tongues;
  Thy sitting upon the Apostles
    in fiery tongues
    after the Ascension.

Thy visiting us to visit the heart,
Thy purifying us,
Thy shining on us, to enlighten us …

Ascension–Pentecost

> I will pour out my spirit upon thy seed ... I am the first and I am the last and beside me there is no God.
>
> Isaiah, chapter 44, verse 6.

> There is one body, and one Spirit ... one hope of your calling, one Lord, one faith, one baptism, one God and Father of all ... who is above all, through all and in you all ...
>
> When he ascended up on high [he] gave gifts to men ...
>
> He that descended is the same also that ascended up far above the heavens that he might fill all things.
>
> St Paul's Epistle to the Ephesians, chapter 4, verses 4–6, 8, 10.

These texts from Isaiah and Ephesians are about unity – the unity of God, and of the old Israel and the New Israel. They are also about the pouring out of the gifts of God's spirit upon all flesh. I say 'on all *flesh*' because Christian faith understands God's self-realization in creation and redemption as *embodiment*. Spirit manifests itself through the material and through humanity, and we handle the Word of life in the Word made flesh.

The fourth chapter of Ephesians – like the creed – outlines the relationship between the God who is one and the God who pours himself out in the universe and in humanity. First we have the affirmation of one God and Father, one Lord, and one baptism into the body of the faithful. Then we have a downward movement as divinity is embodied in our divided and fallen world, pre-eminently in Christ. That coming down has to probe the furthest depths of death and hell before it can rise again, and a New Humanity taken into God. This descent and this ascent releases new and potent gifts on all flesh by pouring out a spirit of unity and power. The fallen and divided condition of mankind is overcome, and the material cosmos itself is renewed as God becomes all in all.

That can be put in a slightly different way. The movement of creation and redemption is from unity to unity through descent into division and death. It is from wholeness to brokenness, and brokenness to wholeness. Through the one God humanity was made 'of one blood' to dwell on the face of the earth. But bloodshed, fratricide and Babel turned one man's hand against another in entrenched misunderstanding and ferocious excommunication.

Salvation, then, is about how to turn things round. It marks out a path of recovery and retrieval; and that depends on the unity and faithfulness of those called to be God's people. First there is the seed of Jacob invoked in Isaiah, and then there is the unity of the New Israel invoked in Ephesians. These are fresh cells generated to counter disastrous disorder. They are fresh irradiations attacking a corrupted body. They are new embodiments of the spirit poured out to join everyone in a bond of peace. According to Isaiah the Gentiles will make their way to the mountain of the Lord and the waste places of Jerusalem will once more be built up. According to the New Testament, Babylon, with its idiom of violence will be overcome by New Jerusalem, with its idiom of peace. When Babylon falls all humanity assembles to join in the universal song.

So we have been presented with an ideal pattern and a joyful prospect, but the world we know shows only modest signs of moving from destruction to re-creation or division to unity. We have, therefore, to face the possibility that faith is just so much pathetic poetry powerless to flesh out its Word. After all, even the Church, proclaimed as the new cell, itself becomes malignant. The tongues of fire poured out in the gift of mutual understanding somehow seem to fall silent. The only plausible prophecy is the one anticipating yet more violence and misery: wars, rumours of wars – and the poor always with us. We appear trapped on Holy Thursday when love's body is stripped by violent men rather than risen again on Easter Day.

How, then, to understand love's impotence? Of course, it is no problem at all for the biogeneticist talking of the undefeated selfish gene and dismissing human beings as just so many 'lumbering robots' hell-bent on survival. Then there are the sociologists and ethologists talking of struggles for dominance by territorial animals, and ruthless competition in pursuit of collective self-interest. And they are right, but is that all? Are the last words 'Nothing but' – nothing but genes or programming or social process? Perhaps we are also creatures cast in a rational mould, mysteriously able to talk of good and evil. The animal that speaks such words not only reacts to stimuli but judges and reflects. Scientific understandings give scant account of this, or of all those other words which mostly take their origin under the aegis of faith, such as generosity and sacrifice, forgiveness and healing. These are the hopeful and inclusive partners to greed and aggrandizement, falsehood and violence. Only poetry and faith, and the poetry of faith, properly encompass these alternative poles of our condition, in all their attraction and their repulsion. T.S. Eliot wrote of 'The great snake ever half awake at the bottom of the pit of the world'. He also wrote of the visible light, at evening or in the morning, light on polished stone or altar, reminding us of the invisible light. Momentarily the clouds unfold to reveal not just tongues but chariots of fire.

These images of hope and glory entered our world with special abandon in the first days of the Gospel, to reposition it. They have taught humankind to attend from time to time to an alternative vision, and to take such opportunities as may come to flesh divine words out. It may be true that most of history is a tale of bad blood, one man's hand against another, but the New Testament reverses that to say we are all one in Christ, who gave his blood rather than taking it. It may also be true that history is dominated by power-seeking, malignant spirits, but the New Testament speaks of a holy spirit lighting on every head as a sign of common speech and the bond of peace. The power of the gospel is in the potential redemption of our vocabulary. Old words, newly charged, have entered into our secular city, powerful but non-violent. Pentecost is the feast of inclusiveness and transparency when the darkened glass becomes the perfect mirror.

So, then, in the world as it is we have tribulation. Yet in the secret history of humanity faith has infiltrated a different vision. That means we are not simply part of the dispersing crowd of Holy Thursday as all the lights go out, but an easter people who light and relight the Paschal candle. In all times and places dominated by the currencies of money and power the different vision recalls us to love's different tender, above all to the embodied love at the heart of the Resurrection, and the universal gift of the peaceable spirit at Pentecost.

The Transfiguration: The Restored Face

And as he prayed, the fashion of his countenance was altered, and his raiment was white and glistening ...

St Luke, chapter 9, verse 29.

Beloved ... we shall be like him; for we shall see him as he is.

First Epistle of St John, chapter 3, verse 3.

I want to set the Transfiguration in the context of the gospels, of the Bible as a whole, and of ourselves and our humankind. So far as the gospels are concerned, this is the end of a phase in the ministry of Christ which was largely centred on Galilee. It is the beginning of a phase largely centred on Jerusalem. Behind lie the teachings and healings and the great feasts on the hillsides inaugurating the Kingdom of God; ahead lie the confrontations in and around Jerusalem, the final Supper, the agony in the Garden, the dereliction of the Cross. Christ stands between two baptisms – there was first the baptism by water in the River Jordan which opened his ministry and there was finally what he called the baptism of his death. And both these baptisms were surrounded by crowds.

But this intermediate moment is quite different. If what was past and what was to come took place in front of crowds, this was intimate and virtually private. An inner circle of three – Peter, James and John – accompanied Christ on the ascent of Mount Tabor. They were the sole witnesses of his glory: 'We beheld his glory; glory as of the only begotten of the Father.' They saw the glory of the Father in the face and the vesture of the Son. 'He that hath seen me hath seen the Father.'

But the three disciples are also aware of something else, and that is the long-term fruition of God's purposes as gradually unveiled in the experience of Israel. The ministry of Christ is now set against the panorama of the whole history of salvation. And perhaps one should say that this history of salvation is only partly connected with ordinary history. Ordinary history took no note of this quiet moment of revelation on a hillside, any more than it took serious note of the crucifixion. This then is (almost) a secret and underground history, turning not so much on noisy events – the clangour of wars and the fall of empires – but on a silent disclosure of a moment of truth. And what was disclosed on Mount Tabor had a connection with two moments of truth in the past: Moses on Sinai and Elijah on Carmel. The beacon that shone out from Mount Tabor picked up light flashed from the beacon on Mount Sinai and from the beacon on Mount Carmel. And as it did so the Law, given by Moses, was completed in a Kingdom of Grace, and all that the prophets – like Elijah – had foretold was fulfilled in Christ. Christ was the consummation of the Law and the Prophets. That is the meaning of this story.

As we look at these three beacons we see certain things in common. The face of Moses shone and so did the face of Christ. Elijah heard a voice, and so too did the three witnesses of the Transfiguration. Through the channels of the senses, by way of sight and sound, comes the knowledge of the presence of God: 'And in the stillness onward came the Lord.' No public verification, but personal testimony, a moment of truth, *face to face*.

So the Transfiguration is a high point in a secret history of experience which, nevertheless, alters the way we see the world and fills us with astonishment. We are amazed: by glory. And this encounter with glory is recorded throughout the entire Bible. For example: The Lord walks in the garden in the cool of the day; as the sun begins to set Jacob sleeps and dreams of a ladder stretching from heaven to earth and angels ascending and descending; as Moses climbs a mountain he sees a bush which burns but is not consumed and realizes this is holy ground; as Elisha is about to receive the mantle of Elijah by the River Jordan he sees the clouds unfold and chariots of fire; as Isaiah enters the temple, he hears the cherubim and seraphim continually crying 'Holy, holy, holy'; as shepherds sit on a hillside by night, they hear the whole host of heaven proclaiming 'Peace on earth'; and – finally – as three women walk through a garden, just as the sun begins to rise, they find that Christ has risen: 'He is not here; he is risen.'

So then, it may be in the cool of the day or by night or at the setting of the sun or at its rising; it may be at the crossing of a river or the ascent of a mountain ... that the Lord is known. These are the moments of truth when the veil of habit and of the everyday vanishes in astonishment and we see things from 'the other side', caught in 'the aspect of eternity'.

That means that what is true of the secret history recorded in the Bible is true of our own history. We too can make a transition to enlightenment and know the presence of the peaceful and of the perfect. We pass from the obscurities of the everyday to moments of clarity and revelation. Most of the time the world is smeared by habit and use, and by the veil of the everyday, but then, often when we least expect it, the mundane alters, the world is transfigured. *All* things, all creation, animate or inanimate, can participate in these times of transfiguration, even though, like Christ, they live in the shadow of death or decay or dissolution. It may be the animation on the face of a child or the repose of venerable age or the moment when the flower opens or the disclosure of a landscape or a stillness at the heart of music.

But among all the signs of God in the whole universe, the human face is special. The divine humanity of Christ was known in his countenance, whether in joy at the transfiguration or in sorrow at his crucifixion. Insofar as we can know anything about the heights and depths of love divine, it is written on the human face and embodied in human form. We ourselves, endowed with our human faces, are already sons and daughters of God, made in his image and receiving and reflecting his love. But in Christ we see the *express* image of the Father, we understand the full glory of the human and realize also that such glory can be ours. As St John himself says: that countenance shows what we may become – changed from 'glory into glory'.

> Beloved, now are we the sons of God, and it doth not yet appear what we shall be but we know that, when he shall appear, we shall be like him, for we shall see him as he is. Amen.

All Saints' Day: Heroes and Martyrs

I will rejoice in Jerusalem and joy in my people; and the voice of weeping shall be no more heard in her.

Isaiah, chapter 65, verse 19.

Seeing we also are compassed about with so great a crowd of witnesses.

Epistle to the Hebrews, chapter 12, verse 1.

I have always admired the roll-call of witnesses to faith in the eleventh chapter of the Epistle to the Hebrews without thinking much about it. The writer of the Epistle magnificently defines faith as the substance of things hoped for, but the more I look at his list of the faithful the more problematic it appears. If we have been to Sunday School we are used to identifying with the war heroes of Israel, but what exactly has Samson to do with 'faith'? His principal exploit was to immolate the Philistines by pulling down the temple on their heads with maximum collateral damage. Of course, I recognise that Samson (like Hercules) has historically been seen as a 'type' of Christ because of the pain he endured in his death, but contemporary Christians, and early Christians too, have always distinguished between heroism in war and death in battle on the one hand and faithful sacrificial love on the other. I think we would be very surprised if the faithful we remembered at All Saints included Richard Lionheart, Bernard Montgomery and Lawrence of Arabia.

So, perhaps, we ought to ask ourselves just why *as Christians* we do not treat war heroes as saints in the way the writer to the Hebrews counted Samson, Gideon, Barak and Rahab the harlot among the faithful. The answer is that the foundation story of Christianity is profoundly reserved about war and violence. In our remembrance of our Saviour's death and passion we celebrate one who 'gave his back to the smiters, and his cheek to them that plucked off the hair'. Unlike Mahomet he neither had a family nor led his people in battle. The difference is crucial. A list of war heroes as exemplars of faith would not worry Ariel Sharon or Osama Bin Laden, but no matter how much we respect other faiths we recoil instinctively when successful mass murderers are accorded the crown of martyrdom. Faith, we believe, is something other than successful violence for a cause. One formulation of this is to say that faith in Islam is programmed for success in the ordinary world, whereas Christianity focusses redemption on an experience of profound suffering, frustration and apparent failure. The reversal of that failure is left entirely in God's hands, *not ours*. No wonder the Koran denies the crucifixion ever happened.

Yet, before we break out in Christian alleluias, let us consider our own practice as well as what we feel and claim to believe. In practice we place redemptive suffering in one compartment of our minds, and the pursuit of just war in another. Particularly when Christianity has partnered the state or the nation Christians have thanked God for success in battle not for failure. Non nobis Domine. So, we are inwardly divided in a way the Islamic world is not, and you can call that a creative tension if you like or, to quote an Islamic specialist of my acquaintance, a pathological inability to face the realities of politics and conflict.

These thoughts crowd my mind because this year we celebrate All Saints while simultaneously remembering the events of September 11th and anticipating the national commemorations of the dead in war on November 11th. These three occasions taken together, focus our minds on the extraordinary tension within Christianity between a suffering love which leaves the future kingdom of righteousness in the hands of God, and of his last judgement, and ourselves making war, whether just or unjust, avoidable or unavoidable, in the name of God or nation or freedom, or all three. The moment *that* situation arises we partly revert to the viewpoint of the ancient Hebrew nation and identify our enemies as the evil ones, as the Archbishop of Canterbury and George Bush have already done. Do not, please, misunderstand me: the events of September 11th were profoundly evil. I am thinking rather of the polarisation of good and evil that follows, with ourselves, our cause, and nation as unequivocally good. And that is problematic for *us* precisely because we are Christians, for whom that kind of unequivocal identification is idolatry. Talking to the Cambridge theologian Daniel Hardy last week he suggested that any Christian understanding of what is happening has to include the identification of that idolatry: God with us. Others may believe it of themselves: for us it is forbidden.

As Christians that is not our only task or our only problem. The New Testament gives us a language in which to understand and speak of redemptive sacrificial love but it has no language for just war, let alone mere warfare, unless we grossly misuse its metaphors of the sword of the spirit and the helmet of salvation. What then are we to do? Confronted by the desolation and suffering of war we feel driven to bring the suffering of the redeemer close to our own. In the London Underground at this moment there are hundreds of British Legion posters which quote 'Greater love hath no man than this, that he lay down his life for his friends'. Quoting the New Testament in that way sets the suffering of the world wars in the context of Christ and his Passion. Nor is that the only difficulty for Christians, because the events of September 11th, though they brought out both heroism and love, resemble the pathetic suffering of Afghan children. They are terrible, yes, but unchosen, in a sense accidental, or as the military vocabulary has it, collateral. There is no Christian language for unchosen collateral immolation, except, of course, the word of hope that death is not conclusive. I believe our response to such kind of death has to be at once Christian and Hebraic. With the Psalmist we cry without relief on account of total waste and loss beyond recall – 'Everything living is altogether vanity' – while we also need to let that other word of hope be spoken, as when they found a metal cross in the rubble of Ground Zero and raised it as a sign and a memorial.

But why do we not feel more acutely the problem and indeed the absence of a Christian response to the terror of contemporary events? It is because we have inherited along with Christianity an enlightened belief in earthly progress whereby providence in the end ensures the arrival of a kingdom of freedom and equality. I heard Beethoven's 'Fidelio' recently and that was precisely its eloquent message framed in the language of Christian enlightenment: grace and light, freedom and justice triumphant. I am not suggesting such a faith is ignoble or even totally deluded. I am saying that if we suppose ourselves its carriers and representatives then we are in danger of self-worship and idolatry. We have also failed to take into account the profound frustration of the human spirit and its vulnerability as placarded in the broken body of Christ. At the service joined in by thousands inside and outside St. Paul's to remember the precious deaths of those who died on the morning of September 11th, the American Ambassador read the words from Isaiah, chapter 65, about loss and restoration. At the conclusion of the service the congregation sang the 'Battle hymn of the Republic':

> As He died to make men holy
> Let us live to make men free,
> While God is marching on

And that was right.

But where we most need to watch our words is not so much in the juxtaposition of Christ and freedom as in the claim that God is marching on. That claim too easily includes the idea that we are specially privy to God's purposes and uniquely preserved from the dust heap of history. What we and the Americans have never experienced is the twentieth century knowledge of nothingness, even though for us in Britain the false optimism of faith died at Passchendaele. By comparison with hundreds of millions of others our enlightened hopefulness has never turned to ashes in our mouth. Our interim difficulties do not compare with their final frustration. Witness all those who died to bring about the false dawns and bitter ends of national socialism and communism.

Visit Berlin today and you find a city materially resurgent and architecturally as resplendent as New York. The fallen towers of 1945, when hardly a stone was left on another, are all cleared away, and only a vestige of the wall of separation remains for remembrance and curiosity's sake. Yet Berlin has been a place where the word of faith was virtually erased by false political hopes, and where it had to be spoken out of total desolation and a final ending. At the heart of Berlin there was once the Kaiser's church, symbol of empire. It is now only a stump. What interior walls remain are covered with pictures of the immolation of 1944 and 1945. By the altar there is a cross recovered from the ruins, just as in New York, in front of which is a single sentence 'Forgive us our trespasses as we forgive them that trespass against us'. Amen.

Part II
Faith's Repertoire

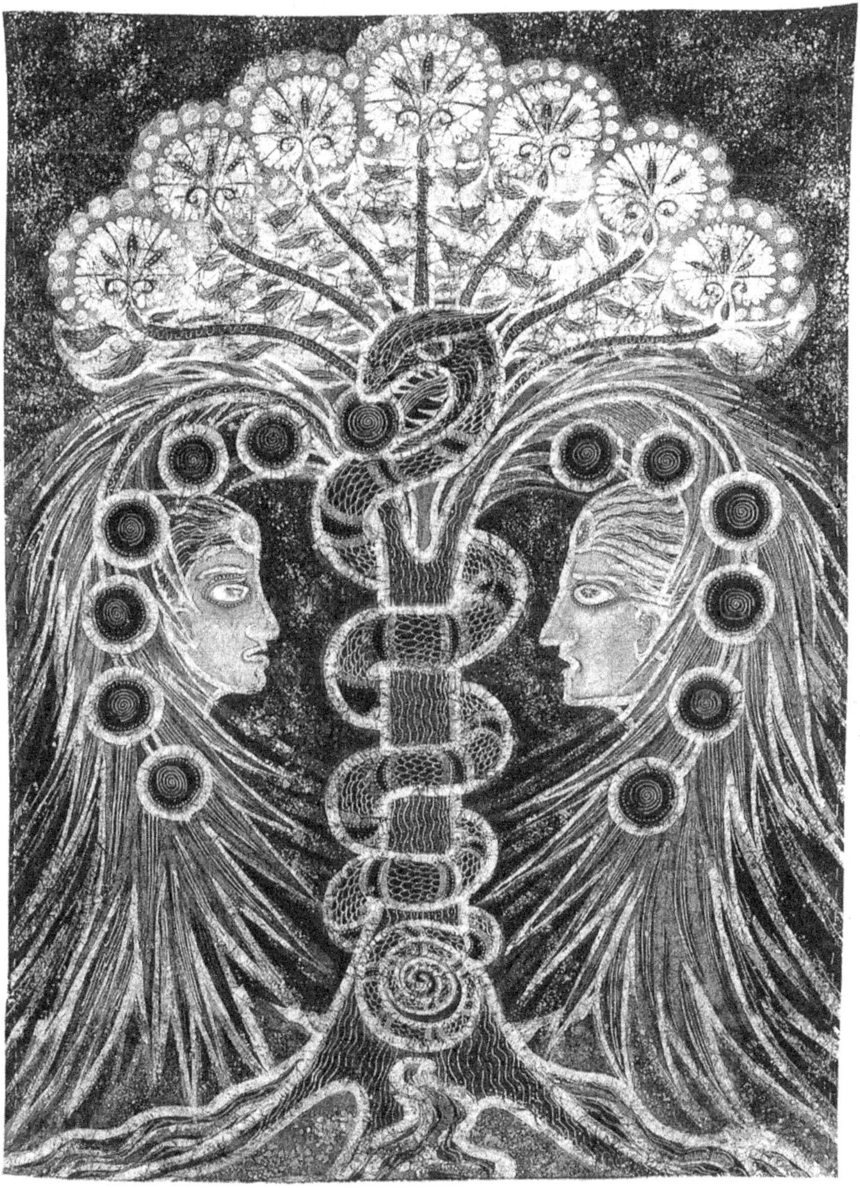

Banner 8 – The Fall

Taken from *The Creation: The Banners of Winchester Cathedral* by Thetis Blacker, Friends of Winchester Cathedral, 2001.

Faith's Repertoire

The language of Christianity as used in the sequence of the liturgy sets an agenda, now to be explored in Part II. That agenda includes the following themes: how is it that the realities of society so rapidly annul and reincorporate the vision of peace and unity; are there ways whereby the seeds of the kingdom, seemingly cast on wasteland, silently burgeon within the secular city; in what ways do we belong simultaneously to the old dispensation and the old city of Jerusalem, with its local loyalties, and to the City of God? This group of themes takes off from the address in Part I on 'From Lakeside to City' and attempts some kind of resolution in 'Peace and Unity' in Part II and in 'War, Peace and Remembrance' in Part III. The issue is fundamental because the idiom of love based on fraternal unity confronts the idiom of violence based on the brokenness, division and fracture at the heart of humanity and human society. It also relates to other issues which are the tension between conventional wisdom as embodied in commonsensical duty and the folly of holy charity, and between proper self-love and losing one's life to find it.

Other themes are: what is it to uncover spiritual truths rather than to discover truths about the world; how can we welcome 'comfortable words' when we are so obviously on our own; how can an overseeing providence cooperate with our freedom; is prayer asking or 'the heart in pilgrimage'; how can we be simultaneously 'miserable sinners' and justified, estranged and accepted; of what is prophecy the antepast and foretaste; how do the angelic and demonic relate to bedevilment and delivery; in what ways is God unimaginable and yet expressly imaged in the human face.

True Comforts

Is your religion no comfort to you?

(Book of Job, chapter 4, verse 6 *NEB*).

Certain passages in the Bible taken on their own seem to suggest that the chosen People of God will prosper if they keep his commandments, and that the individual man of God will prosper if he keeps God's law. These passages, for example, in Deuteronomy (chapter 28) and in Job (chapter 4) assert that God's sovereignty is realized in the well-being of the just nation and the virtuous man. Of course, from the rest of the Book of Job it is clear this cannot be so, since the whole plot turns on the mystery of undeserved suffering. The psalmist underlines the same point when he complains, 'the wicked flourish as the green bay tree', and in the gospels Jesus rejects any idea of a connection between wrong-doing and suffering or misfortune. That means that any answer to the question 'Is your religion no comfort to you?' depends (as always) on what we mean by comfort. If 'the comfort of the Holy Spirit' is not insurance against calamity then what is it?

Let me straightaway put on one side the notion in Deuteronomy that the righteous nation will be 'always the head and not the tail'. From the Christian perspective the People of God are citizens of a heavenly Jerusalem beyond any nation, or tribe or tongue, and attempts to see so-called Christian nations, like Victorian Britain or now the USA, as God's elect are blasphemous nonsense.

Yet though we may be very clear there is no direct connection between godliness and national power or prosperity, it is still possible to talk as if there were some sort of divinely ordained link between individual virtue and material well-being. Indeed, there are plenty of contemporary Christians ready to answer the question 'Is your religion no comfort to you?' with an upbeat gospel of health and wealth. To be fair, these Christians could point to some evidence that virtue, moderation, self-discipline and membership of a faith community contribute to long life, well-being and happiness. I have certainly known several marvellously gifted people who died early on account of excess, desperation – and isolation. Today all over the developing world tens of millions of impoverished Pentecostals claim raised standards of living in every sense, and witness to what they would call miracles of spiritual and bodily healing following a new life in Christ. And it may well be that authoritative assurance of acceptance, forgiveness and infinite worth in the eyes of God, includes a restoration of the whole person, body and soul. Many millions are at one and the same time spiritually bound and bodily crippled, and they can be dramatically unbound and buoyed up by the care and prayer of the community of faith. There are also spiritually gifted people whose 'virtue' given out in blessing, infuses new life and hope, else the gospels themselves make little sense. The gospels also make clear in teaching and in practice that suffering is not the will of God.

So then, for many charismatic Christians spiritual renewal offers present comfort in the world here and now. Theirs is a 'God of power and might' who liberates from oppression and depression. A 'big God' empowers. The trouble is that such a faith can turn our relationship to God into magical thinking based on a kind of contract. When God doesn't deliver spiritual, bodily or political liberation we blame ourselves or else we lose faith. Our God is then revealed as a magical projection of our own infantile omnipotence, under contract to our special needs and hopes. We say 'What have I done to deserve this?' when after all every day brings fresh news of hundreds of millions besides ourselves suffering through no fault of their own.

How then may we distinguish between false and true comforts of the spirit? I take off from a personal illustration, because not so long ago my eldest son was taken suddenly into hospital with a suspected malign growth. When it turned out benign the human instinct was to say 'Thank God', and yet clearly if the growth had been malign I would not have blamed God – though that was precisely one of the responses suggested to Job. And the reason why I would not blame God is clear enough. The processes of nature constitute an orderly and neutral arena beyond magical manipulation, otherwise scientific knowledge and its remedies would be bedevilled by the random and inexplicable. God is not a random infusion into causality on the cue of prayer, and that has implications not only for what we mean by prayer but for what it means to say, 'I believe in God'. Speaking only for myself I do not think prayer a way to prod lazy omnipotence and sleepy omniscience into proving itself by an unpredictable display of power; and moreover the God I believe in is not some vacuous general explanation for the world tacked on where other more specific explanations stop. I also sometimes wonder if it might help our thinking to imagine the deathliness of an alternative universe in which neither growth nor deterioration occurred, and contingency and the anxieties of time did not exist. The God I *do* believe in is a mysterious sign of a transformation and a fullness with which we align ourselves in faith and hope. Our alignment is the eastward turn we make to the source of light, re-enacted in miniature every time we light a candle.

What then might the true comforts of faith be? The eastward turn, if I can call it that, the lighting of the candle, is our gesture of gratitude and wonder for the givenness of life. It signifies our readiness to 'greet' every manifestation of glory whether in creation or in human inspiration, from Bach to a child's first scribble. We pray *Veni Creator Spiritus*: 'Come Creator Spirit.' That also means going below the surface noise of self to a different presence and another kind of attention. The Book of Revelation speaks of a door opening in heaven and a trumpet sounding. In the gospels, Jesus practised the presence of God by retirement from the crowd to the hillside, the wilderness and the solitary place. It was there that angels ministered to him as they did also to Elijah.

But then from this restorative silence and solitary communion we return to a journey made in company, where we are dependent not on angels but on human ministries of grace, on blessing and absolution, acceptance and release, comfort and counsel, judgement and reconciliation. As far as we are able we undertake a conversation in the bond of peace and we are freely fed by the bread of heaven placed in our hands without money and without price. We stand 'under the cross' as the saving sign of a strength perfected in weakness, and retell the story of God identified with humanity both in death's dereliction and birth's epiphany.

One Holy Week my wife and I were staying on Lake Como, and in the village church we listened to the story of how the Living Word was left derelict, silenced by violence and death. Yet in that pit of violence and evil faith dares to pitch salvation's tent. On Good Friday the body of Christ was carried around the village in mourning for the extinction of the light. Then early on Easter Sunday all the bells rang up and down the lake to say the last word was not, after all, with the powers of death and hell. And so, if we can bear it, the true comfort of the spirit is to pass through the silence and the failure of the light to the renewal of the flame and a fresh advent of the tongues of fire.

Loss and Realization of Life

> He that loseth his life for my sake shall find it.
>
> St. Matthew's Gospel, chapter 10, verse 39.

> Therefore are we buried with him by baptism unto death: that like as Christ was raised up from the dead by the glory of the Father, even so we also should walk in newness of life.
>
> St. Paul's Epistle to the Romans, chapter 6, verse 4.

This gospel from St Matthew is part of the preaching commission of Jesus as the disciples were about to take the word to the people of Israel, and it contains many uncomfortable words, some remote from our situation. We are not about to leave home to announce the kingdom and clearly that option has only ever been the special vocation of a few. In any case we always have to remember that the one who said, 'If thine eye offend thee pluck it out' was a master of hyperbole as well as paradox. If that wasn't pretty obvious there would be more self-mutilated fundamentalists about than seems to be the case.

The paradox of our text is common both to Jesus and to Paul and it is that enslavement to sin leads to spiritual death whereas death to sin leads to life and liberty. You can call this a part of Christian moral psychology because we are asked to understand the atonement, enacted once for all on Calvary's hill, not only as history but also as the inward law of every spiritual biography. Like the cross the spiritual law is stark. Place yourself at the centre of everything and your universe implodes; give yourself away in generous love and your universe expands infinitely to the resurrection and the life. In the words of Jesus, fear above all else the loss of your soul and its integrity and you have nothing else to fear. Seen in this perspective Christianity embodies an unavoidable truth about first things, the language of priorities. It is the divine self-emptying and dying into life of incarnate love.

We might call this saying about losing your life to find it the first law of spiritual dynamics, proved on the pulses because it works. However, like all profound laws it is prone to misunderstanding and misuse. I mean, for example, that for someone whose life has been devastated this is no recommendation or guarantee of emotional immunity or even of spiritual poise. Christianity is not Roman stoicism improved with good stories, though I've known Anglicans who thought it was. Jesus himself was angry, distressed and indignant, and when he entered on his own time of troubles he wept over Jerusalem, and in the garden, shed (as it were) great drops of blood.

Nor does this first law of the spirit mean we are always to suppress our needs or humbly refrain from speaking our mind or seeking truth and justice. This is no invitation to a kind of manipulation of others by mute exposure of wounds or conspicuously playing the victim. When Christianity turns upside down the assumptions of the world by declaring the lord of all the servant of all it is not recommending we all become doormats. What the commandment to love others *as* ourselves must mean is that we scrutinize our own self-love as suspiciously and rigorously as we scrutinize the self-love of others. In Paul's phrase we ought 'in honour' to prefer one another.

Very well then, and what a relief, because we have virtually scaled Christianity back again to proverbial wisdom and British common sense. We have a truth about human pride and self-concern such as struck Gulliver when he came back from life among the rational Houyhnhnms and was shaken by the puffed-up stupidity of humankind. The pride which Gulliver condemned was ludicrous unreason.

But *where now* the dramatic New Testament contrast between enslavement to sin and glorious liberty, the passage through the baptism of death to the resurrection and the life? I suggest that requires us to explore further Christian moral psychology, above all the unmentionable doctrines of the Fall and Hell. Proverbially pride comes before a fall, but for Christianity pride *is* the fall, and our chronic and anxiety-ridden self-concern becomes an easy way to a serious hell. Without noticing it we follow the natural inclination, which is the natural declination down to hell and hopelessness. Hell's prison works on us by a subtle acclimatization to its ways. It becomes our unchallenged normality in which we are so eaten up by pride and consumed by envy we cannot even imagine, much less desire, a solid joy or a lasting pleasure. We deny ourselves joy because we treat others as so much there just for our convenience that we no longer communicate with them as human beings. We have so confined our gaze to self-worship that our human faces grow estranged and the imprint of God's image on us is eaten away.

If only we could lift our eyes to a light radiating from another centre than self, our distracted 'I' would find its true place in the perspective of incarnate love. Where our gaze is, there will our likeness be also. Self-love self-defeats. We could discover that white stone of Revelation which is marked with our true name. By the disciplined practice of the divine presence we could recover our own presence of soul and go out with joy to a world marvellously made up of God's good creatures. We might even enjoy that freedom of mastery such as comes in any sphere when we yield to the nature of the material and give way to the character of the art.

But why do I speak so tentatively of what we might or could do to enlighten our self-imposed confinement? The answer again lies in a Christian moral psychology, one which is as rigorous in its realism about our corruption and incapacity as it is in its demands.

What can release us? cries Paul. Why is it, realistically, that we come again and again acknowledging our manifold sins and wickedness and saying, 'We are not worthy so much as to gather up the crumbs' under God's table? Has God trapped us between moral demand and chronic incapacity, expecting perfection while knowing full well that we are as dust?

Happily there is a second law of spiritual dynamics to complement the first, and a second reading of the cross offering comfortable words to temper the uncomfortable ones. And where one braces the other relaxes. According to the first law, the first reading, the cross on Calvary's hill is a stark warning of the terrible cost to be borne in attempting a difficult ascent. If our self is buried with Christ in the baptism of his death then we are raised with him in the loving communion of all the sons and daughters of God. According to the second law, the second reading, the cross is a promising sign of grace to cover all our sin and incapacity. God has covered for us, picked up the terrible cost on his own account making minus plus. No matter how alien or estranged we have become, living so long in a far country, God has already come close. He is there before us, putting on us the robe of acceptance, assuring us that our place at table as worthy guest is already prepared.

The table overflows with goodness and mercy.

So we may sit and eat.

The Prophetic: Antepast and Foretaste

Whoever receives a prophet as a prophet shall receive a prophet's reward.
St Matthew's Gospel, chapter 10, verse 41.

What is prophecy and what is the role of the prophet and the prophet's reward?

Prophecy discerns signs of the times already with us as it looks for restoration and moral governance in the good providence and good time of God. In dramatic close-up it forth-tells our sifting by judgement and our consolation by grace. Prophecy projects a frame for the hope of things unseen which brings us through the times of trial until our feet stand again within the gates of Zion. Through prophecy the penury of our contemporary regime is measured against the inclusive scope of a divine generosity. In that day, perhaps soon and with our cooperation, there will be a fresh advent embodying truth and love. In that world each and all sit under fig trees and forget the arts of war in emblematic landscapes surrounding visionary cities. Creation rules, as alien is made citizen, slave made son, and those redeemed from deep estrangement join in one to hymn the sacred name. *Jubilate*.

Seen this way the prophet is the presenting edge of crisis and the terrors built into recovery: the depredations and corruptions of power, the expropriation of the weak and disregarded, the expulsion of the stranger – as well as the end of the Unrighteous and of the Lie. Remember Blake's picture of Nebuchadnezzar, maddened, naked and driven from men, who ate grass till his hairs grew like eagles' feathers and his nails like birds' claws.

In a premillennial year one thinks of how the repertoire of prophecy has been enlarged by what Isaac Watts called the opera of apocalypse: scenarios of ages and stages, mystic numbers, heraldic beasts, signs and seals. Centre stage is Last Battle and Last Judgement. In the Last Battle prophecy imagines the joys and sorrows of that terrible field where stands the Lion of Judah and where lies the wounded King. In the Last Judgement faith attests the moment of truth against the Lie. Everything is exposed to the light with the arrival of the heavenly city, Philadelphia.

Behind these landscapes of the imagination lurks the potent myth of our separation, our melancholy and our longing for union. Somehow, perhaps by a primal disease of consciousness or fell effect of obdurate pride the way forward and the way back stay barred, leaving us stranded on middle ground, partly knowing and darkly seeing. We suspect some usurpation by opaque and contrary powers, a principle of perverse dominion, a violent massing of malignant energies. Nevertheless, our prayer is still for a coming kingdom. We still project a vision of the Lamb's bridal party assembled at the city gate and of the opening up of the crystal fountains. On that day, says the Book of Revelation, the mystery of God should be finished because we shall truly know and directly see.

Well, in all that I am trying to evoke a repertoire of transforming signs, built up in ancient Israel, over two and a half millennia ago under impact of threat and exile, and massively revised to encompass Christian experience. Clearly the deployment of that repertoire turns on the nature of time, including time past as well as future time. So I need to conclude with reflections on prophecy and time. As a partly open future slips by into a seemingly inert past the fluid medium of prophecy sets hard in papyrus, text and settled interpretation. The dead past continues to speak in a present voice but so often to shore up present powers. Passionate outcries turn monumental and Ezekiel appears in the Sistine chapel. The Dove of the Spirit is taken on board to stabilize the Barque of Christ; and William Blake had a place set aside in the Millennium Dome.

Yet however stabilized as monuments or pulled into line as precursors the old images are in perpetual motion, revivified, reanimated. Though rendered immobile in mural or mosaic we can still scan the holy cities, sacred and delectable mountains, excoriating deserts, and rivers of life. Realistically, of course, we always face the terror of random oscillation and chaos. And humanely we bind over the forward look of annunciation and advent in benign liturgical rotation, else there would be no sacred vessels in which to recollect hope. Still prophecy reactivates vision. It is our orientation to purpose and fruition, our eastward turn to Jerusalem.

Think how prophecy animates the New Testament and how embedded it is in the reception, identification and understanding of Christ. Simeon and Anna, for example, the venerable representatives of the old order, prophetically identified Christ, and received the prophets' reward. For our Lord himself the voice of prophecy, especially Isaiah, was alive and contemporary. In that text he found his place in a genealogy of messengers, often like himself in coming in from remote margins of mountain or desert, and as often rejected: the prophet's reward. He located a pathway marked out from exodus to liberty, passing through Jordan, testing in the wilderness, a new law on the mount, an entry into Jerusalem.

On the Mount of Transfiguration, Moses and Elijah, law and prophecy, joined him on either side, conversing across time, new completing old without cancellation. When in his own person he inaugurated the kingdom with beatitude and benediction thousands gathered to receive their living bread. As disciples gathered for a last supper all types and shadows had their ending in a new testament which was foretaste and antepast of heaven. After the terrible baptism of Christ's death his disciples renewed their communion with him through the invocation of a name, the recognition of a gesture or greeting, through a presence realized in breaking of bread or eating of fish.

In a way the world after the resurrection stayed and stays exactly as it was: our gaze partial, our environment opaque and light-resistant, history full of dead ends, reversals, sidetracks. The real presence of God stays hidden under fragmented forms and signs of brokenness. Yet as faith tells and retells the story, the central redoubt of the Last Enemy – death, violence and the annihilation of hope by violent death has been captured, turned round, faced forward. We recover fullness through the brokenness. We enter boldly the holy place through the standing of our mortally wounded king. It is from the riven rock, struck violently by the rod, that there flows a grace to cover us from head to foot and by a 'pure ablution' cleanse the stain of the world, making it new.

Kinds of Discovery

You shall know the truth and the truth shall set you free.
St John's Gospel, chapter 8, verse 32.

What is the relation between what we 'discover' in the university and what we 'discover' by faith? There was a time, half a millennium ago, when the two kinds of discovery were closely intertwined. The motto of the University of Oxford, 'The Lord is my light' reminds us of centuries when the metaphor of light was not divided between secular enlightenment and religious illumination. Up to quite recently universities mingled spires and libraries, seminars and seminaries.

Now the relationship of the two kinds of discovery is strained, and some argue they are incompatible. Those who insist on incompatibility hold there is only one kind of discovery, which is science, and faith is no more than antique superstition. You find nothing out when you enter a sacred building, because it houses no more than a museum of myths and past mistakes. Even worse, you may contaminate your mind with error. Faith carries forward on the books all the false trails followed by humanity until such people as Roger Bacon and later Francis Bacon discovered scientific method.

Even if we set aside this secular dogmatism there remain questions about the place of faith in a university, and about the relation between different kinds of discovery. After all, one faith differs from another, so what once united people now divides them. The sheer variety of faiths stands in vivid contrast to the shared criteria of the scholarly enterprise. Moreover, many people today cannot even imagine overarching meanings and purposes.

Of course, the university is not divided up simply between two opposed or alternative modes, science and faith. In between there is much variable territory, such as the project of understanding society or the humanities. Indeed, it often seems that the pursuit of the humanities resembles the engagement of faith because it can explore our interior worlds. Literature in particular seems to offer secular paths to salvation by moral criticism, enlarged sympathy, coming to terms with ourselves, enrichment of experience. The question then becomes: is this cultivation of self at all equivalent to the commitment of self required by faith?

Those who implicitly answer 'Yes' regard the university as our contemporary multi-cultural church for self-cultivation as well as for all the different modes of understanding. There are many booths, side-altars for devotees. Only the axis, the orientation, the inclusive arch, is missing. The arch has been declared broken and the space of the whole and the holy empty.

In this fragmented 'university as new church' it is maybe painting and music which lie closest to the old neighbourhood of faith: by entering into ecstasy and terror, and by offering means for the outpouring of being and tranquillity of soul. Art galleries are our remaining sacred space; the contemporary iconostasis screening the holy. Yet still there is no governing iconography or images grouped around the redemptive story. You just enter a hushed antechamber of the spirit, where people loosely congregate, each preoccupied with an image, as if caught in an attitude of vestigial prayer.

Concert halls are the remaining Sunday service for many who dismiss Genesis as mere myth, suppose faith suppressed eroticism, think Christmas for children, and suspect the glory of conscious being reducible to genes and circuitry. Music is their ecstasy without words, technique in thrall to soul, transfiguration of self and world, reconciliation of opposites, shared communion through pure resonance.

And it looks as if composers often agree. Even today after the collapse of the arch this resonance or sounding forth gravitates to the texts of faith as if they alone contain a matching power. Not only believers but composers with no faith 'to speak of' somehow find faith to compose with. The explicit prayer of the Church gives back a location and name to the unmarked landscape of the spirit, a chance to relearn the neglected language of another country.

Meanwhile there are others, including some ministers of the church, who are discontented with text, hesitant before the seemingly settled certainties of creeds. They revert to a silent prayer or lighting of candles. For them gestures of blessing and of giving come easier than articulate faith and hope. The space of the whole and holy, oriented to God, the source of all being, simply allows clandestine inwardness room to be. Miracle, healing and epiphany are mutely acknowledged in spite of all waste, deterioration and final loss.

So this space with its strange inclusiveness – in the temple or in us – what *is* it *for*? It invites us to cross a threshold beyond the rational need to manipulate, dissect, calibrate, or observe. Across that threshold observation gives place to insight, object becomes emblem, and the givens of analysis manifest themselves as pure gift. In such space a sign language focusses vision, because without focus vision vanishes, though it is not its nature to impose itself in the way propositions and observations impose themselves. Signs invite us to *dis*cover or *un*cover what is meant by disintegration and integrity, frustration and fulfilment, chaos and order, evil and good, scarcity and plenitude, absence and presence. Horizons open up, with pointers of deformation and markers of transformation. A sacrament is a marker of transformation, and a way station for refreshment, where we absorb the elements of earth – water, bread, wine, as tangible metaphors of renewal, recreation, resurrection. About the nature of resurrection we barely know anything at all. All we might hope to discover is the gift of a Word of Promise to do with a truthfulness which is able 'to set us free'.

Justification of Fallen Creatures

> The heart is deceitful above all things and desperately wicked.
>
> Jeremiah 17, verse 9.

> Therefore as by the offence of one judgement came upon all men to condemnation; even so by the righteousness of one the free gift came upon all men unto justification of life.
>
> St. Paul's Epistle to the Romans, chapter 5, verse 18.

These texts concern the Fall of Man and the reality of evil. If I were an evangelical preacher of the kind I sometimes encounter in the United States I would engage in a blow-by-blow encounter with Paul in his titanic struggle to deliver the message of Grace Triumphant. But that kind of engagement with a whole passage is not possible in the office of Mattins. What I can do is to put forward my own minor encounter with Paul's theme and with the great oppositions informing his text: life and death, righteousness and condemnation, reconciliation and enmity, justification and judgement, grace and sin. Underlying all these, of course, are the two mightiest oppositions: Fallen Man and Redeeming Man. All else turns around Fall and Redemption. We are fallen and we are redeemed.

When you are dealing with the great themes of the Faith you should begin with the obvious. The Fall of Man refers to the solidarity in evil of all the sons of Adam and all the daughters of Eve. The universal taint and the unavoidable contagion admit of no exception, bond nor free, male nor female, Jew nor Gentile. All are inextricably one in the old Adam, our representative man. All, as Scripture affirms, have come short of the glory of God. 'The heart is deceitful above all things', says Jeremiah, 'and desperately wicked.'

Of course, there are people who think it antique or unscientific or just harshly judgemental to speak of wickedness. Confronted with the long tally of crime from murdering Cain to the shooting of a six-month-old baby by a terrorist, they may think it adequate to speak of maladjustment or poor integration or even pathology. This can seem to imply that there are some people, perhaps most of us in fact, who are quite well adjusted, nicely integrated, thank you, and in excellent psychological health. But that is not what the Bible says. It speaks grimly of our universal solidarity in sin.

Pathological is, of course, a word which sounds scientific and looks medical. Not only is it a long way from any idea that we share a solidarity in sin but it can suggest that we live in a modern world where moral judgement as such is out of date. We are no longer allowed to characterize actions as right or wrong, good and bad. It all comes down to biology or if not biology to culture and different cultural standards. And yet that very word 'pathological' easily loses its scientific reference and becomes an undercover moral judgement. Confronted by something genuinely horrifying we say, 'That is quite pathological'. In that way we still sound scientific, even perhaps medical, but at root and at heart the judgement we make is moral. That is *wrong*. And that suggests to me that in our human speech there is no way of cutting out the moral reference or eliminating moral judgement and discrimination. You cannot jettison the fundamental human vocabulary of Good and Evil. The Good and the Bad are perennial. We *have* to say that some things are evil, depraved, reprehensible, wicked, absolutely unacceptable and just plain *wrong*. People do things they ought not, they pursue ends that are unworthy and unjust. You may, if you like, characterize machine-gunning a baby as 'pathological'. But this language will not do. It does not measure up. We need to say and must say that it is 'desperately wicked'.

We need then, as moral beings, speaking and judging in a moral world, to do two things. We have first to use our moral sense, our conscience, to decide on what is worthwhile and what is unworthy. We have to apportion precise blame *justly*, so far as is possible. We have to learn to discern and exercise intelligent carefulness in our relations with ourselves and others. We have to be care-full, we have to consider what actions and ends lead to human flourishing. And that is for ourselves and for others all part of living responsibly in a moral world and honouring virtue whenever we encounter it. But we have, secondly, to acknowledge that even the virtuous man or virtuous woman is enmired, enmeshed, and entrapped in the profound solidarity of evil. And this is not a matter of being obsessed with guilt, our own or anybody else's, or of some perverse pleasure in denigrating our humanity, but of soberly recognizing where and what we are. Evil sucks all into an interconnected web from which none of us seem able to escape. There is a blood-soaked and bloated spider at the centre of that web. 'The heart is deceitful above all things and desperately wicked.' This is the common human inheritance of an equality and a fraternity in serfdom, a partnership in all imperfection and in the wrongs of man. It is what Christianity calls the Fall and what Pascal called the Misery of Man, *Grandeur et Misère de L'Homme*.

How then shall we escape? The answer is in the oddest way possible by placing ourselves under judgement, under what St Paul terms 'the law'. Unless you put yourself under judgement there is no relief. Of course, there are dangers in this as in everything: you can become obsessed with moral scrutiny and crazily censorious towards yourself. I am not talking about stoking up the fires of guilt so that we can all stare morosely into our own flaming hells. I am simply inviting an assessment of our condition under the law. Each one of us has taken part in the primal crime of Cain – taken part inasmuch as we have diminished the life of others and smothered their search for life and space and room. And this participation in the hand of Cain is not necessarily quite direct. It is often a slightly indirect but terrible consequence of seeking something we perceive as worthwhile: the terrorist did not *directly* seek the life of the baby. Yet he murdered her. He murdered her.

So, then, we are all caught up, though not by absolutely direct culpability and not by absolutely clear-cut intention, in an inch by inch loss of life and in an inch by inch implication in death. We pass on and receive the mortal contagion in a spiral of deadly reciprocity.

It is as the consequences of 'sin's' contagion unravel over years, and even aeons of time since Adam's Fall and Cain's malicious envy, that we can begin to assess our participation in the Fall, in general as humans, in particular by the faultiness in ourselves. We grasp in a moment of terror the depth of our implication: we are *in it*, up to the hilt. We find ourselves and place ourselves face to face with the one – or the many – whom we have broken or helped to break. And as we look on what our brokenness has broken and on what our disfigurement has disfigured, then and only then are we broken enough to be healed and restored. It is the marvellous and relentless pressure of truth which affords us ultimate relief.

'They shall look on Him whom they have pierced.' It is in that exchange of looks that the law of sin and death is put into reverse. 'There is, therefore, *no condemnation* to them that are in Christ.' The law no longer applies; the condemnation no longer stands; the death sentence is abrogated; the fallen are lifted clean out of the pit and the naked are clothed head to foot in righteousness. Now we have found the ground wherein we stand:

> For since by man came death
> By man came also the resurrection from the dead
> For as in Adam all die
> Even so in Christ shall all – shall *all* be made
> alive.

On Faith and Being Made Whole

give unto us the increase of faith

Collect for the fourteenth Sunday after Trinity.

If ye be led by the Spirit ye are not under the law ... the fruit of the Spirit is love, joy, peace ... goodness, faith ...

St. Paul's Epistle to the Galatians, chapter 5, verses 18 and 22.

Arise, go thy way: thy faith hath made thee whole

St. Luke's Gospel, chapter 17, verse 19.

It occurs to me, looking at these three texts that faith is *the* distinctive word of the New Testament, as much as love and far more so than hope. Faith occurs once or twice in the Old Testament, perhaps two hundred times in the New. So if you think there is nothing new in the New Testament you are mistaken.

Yet people use the word faith to mean many different things. Sometimes it means belief, or those positions or propositions you feel plausible and credible. At other times it means setting aside the language of obligation, test, right and claim in favour of love, joy, confidence and trust. The law is to be honoured as a guide to conduct but broken in its power to condemn. I want now to speak against faith as belief and credibility and in favour of faith as confidence and trust.

Of course, I personally have nothing against credibility. I simply notice it is of no interest whatever to the New Testament. If the New Testament had put forward hypotheses in order to recommend their credibility it would long ago have been falsified as out-of-date science. Instead it remains true yesterday and today because it is a story beginning and ending in annunciations. 'Hail Mary' said the angel, 'All Hail' said the risen Lord.

There are no experiments in the New Testament to demand our belief but only manifestations of glory to attract our wonder. The glory of God 'shines forth' in a human face. Christ is not commended by compelling reasons because compulsion would violate our freedom. We are left only with the reasons of the heart: 'Is it nothing to you all ye that pass by?' Faith addresses each one of us by name.

In our everyday lives we manipulate things and people, assessing price and measuring consequences but as Christians we simply give thanks for tokens of love placed freely in our hands. What we are offered is precious but has no price; the gifts of God overflow and they have no measure. Here and now meeting at the common table we come not to be informed but to kneel.

But – you may say – if Christianity cannot offer compelling reasons for belief does it not stand for the moral law and provide wise precepts for our obedience, happiness and human flourishing? Yes, it does. Does it not commend truthful witness, respect for what is another's, reverence for life, and honour to whom honour due? Yes, it does. This is where Old and New Testaments agree. 'Happy is the man whose delight is in the law of the Lord' says the Psalmist; and St. Paul commends the virtues of love, joy, peace and goodness. True, the new law of Christ differs profoundly from rules and observances because it offers instead blessings on those who seek the kingdom. All the same, the law remains the foundation of humane living and we are bound to duty and to discernment. Without the law we are 'like brute beasts that have no understanding'. No law, no grace; no offence no forgiveness. Why else should the commandments precede the holy communion or the tablets of the law stand over the table of grace?

Nevertheless, the New Testament links law with death. Because of the sin which so easily besets us we cannot meet the law's demands and are chronically in default. Because we cannot call back the lost time the wrongs and debts of the past can never be cancelled. Our hearts fail us because there is nothing to be gained by a rescheduling of the debt when what we most need is the debt wiped out and the sins forgiven. Our standing with others and with the world about us may be performance-related, and often a matter of 'nicely calculated less or more', but before God and the deep things of the Spirit we seek acceptance not assessment. We want 'the Spirit to bear witness with our spirit' that we are the children of God, and to be accounted righteous. No wonder Paul wrote 'There is therefore no condemnation to them that are in Christ', or that Luther spoke of faith alone and grace alone, or that we come now to the table 'not trusting in our own righteousness' but 'by faith and with thanksgiving'.

That is Catholic as well as Reformed teaching. Probably you remember the gothic and renaissance pictures of Christ which show him rising triumphant not only over the death of the body but over the death that comes by the law. Christ rises from a tomb from which the stone has already been removed. For the fathers that stone was the tablet of the law. By his rising again Christ abolished the letter to establish the spirit.

So, then, faith cannot be expressed either by compelling reasons or moral achievements. It comes instead as a new wine which breaks through the old bottles; and we are invited to receive it without money and without price. 'For the law came by Moses but grace and truth by Jesus Christ'.

Les Murray's recently published poems, entitled 'Learning Human', are dedicated 'to the glory of God'. Listen to part of one of them entitled 'The Say-but-the-Word Centurion Attempts a Summary'

> If he is risen, all are children of a most high real God
> or something even stranger called by that name
> who knew to come and be punished for the world.
>
> To have knowledge of right after that, is to be in the wrong.
> Death came through sight of the law.

The poem continues enigmatically with the words 'regained excels kept he taught', which means I think, that what you keep, whether it is the law or your innocence, your talents or much treasure, belongs to you by nature. But what you regain after loss and breakage comes to you by faith and by grace. Christianity is not necessary for those who stay at home, safe in the father's house and shielded from waste and loss, who are, after all, secure in their reward. Only the son returning from a long sojourn in a far country can be robed in righteousness and invited to the great feast of reconciliation. This is the law written on the tablets of the heart, more beautiful and more terrible than anything written on tablets of stone. According to love, it is only when you have yourself felt the wound that you can be healed, reconciled, and made whole. Think of all those people in the towers of the World Trade Center who knowing they were about to die wanted to give only one message, 'I love you'.

> E'er since, *by faith*, I saw the stream
> Thy flowing wounds supply.
> Redeeming love has been my theme,
> And shall be till I die.

'Arise, go thy way: thy *faith* hath made thee whole'.

Duty and Divine Charity

Fear God and keep his commandments, for this is the whole of duty of man.
Ecclesiastes, chapter 12, verse 13.

For I, even I, am he that blotteth out thy transgressions.
Isaiah, chapter 44, verse 25.

Anthony Harvey, the distinguished New Testament scholar, has suggested that in the New Testament we have a pithy wisdom which was part of the shared moral apprehension of the ancient world. Here in the New Testament is no utterly distinctive diet, but rich common food, shared among the Romans and the Greeks and 'the barbarians' and, for that matter, grasped today by most ordinary folk. In the New Testament, we have pithy stories, short sharp sayings which land in the solar plexus, maxims which heighten and summarize our moral experience. Even when the sayings of the New Testament seem to overturn our world, we are being taught that moral apprehension is simultaneously paradoxical and profoundly ordinary. At one moment our Lord takes one arm of a paradox and dramatizes it; the next moment he turns to the viewpoint of ordinary moral common sense. You know the law: so keep it.

No wonder then there is a continuity between Jesus and the great rabbis, like Hillel, and with the wisdom literature of Proverbs, Ecclesiastes and Ecclesiasticus. No wonder that when Christianity most naturally and easily communicates with modern mankind, especially in England, it does so in terms of this permanent treasure of moral experience and sensitivity. Much follows from such an easy relationship with perennial wisdom. We do not have to apologize for the presence of Christianity in schools and evacuate the moral content of education as a kind of embarrassing extra or improper imposition. We are, in this area at least, saying little more than the average moral man, woman, or child wants to hear and should hear. No doubt there is a difficult margin of disagreement, especially over matters like divorce and abortion, but the shared bedrock is vast. The citizens of Britain are hungry for an affirmation of moral fundamentals, about truthfulness and faithfulness, prudence and constancy, discipline and self-giving, upright dealing and charity. Politically and personally they want these decencies upheld. At the heart of this is nothing less than Christian caritas, 'the most excellent gift of charity' meaning: the right spirit informing our moral being and our affections.

Of course, wisdom can turn into sententiousness such as you encounter on speech days, or in Lord Chesterfield's letters, or read on eighteenth-century monuments. But it is part of wisdom precisely to avoid this corruption of the way we commend conscientiousness.

Something of this wisdom of the people and wisdom for the people was conveyed for four and a half centuries in the *Book of Common Prayer*. I have just now opened my Prayer Book at random and I immediately find injunctions to sobriety, hospitality and good stewardship, as well as a commendation of fervent charity. The ten commandments which once so properly framed the holy communion and were taught to every child, are simply summaries of the highest moral wisdom.

The most perfect expression of what I have in mind happens to be set out in the Epistle for the Fifth Sunday after Trinity: It recommends the right way for those who would 'love life' and 'see good days'. Listen to it in the grave and mellow music of an earlier English:

> Be ye all of one mind, having compassion one of another, love as brethren, be pitiful, be courteous; not rendering evil for evil, or railing for railing; but contrariwise blessing; knowing that ye are thereto called, that ye should inherit a blessing. For he that *will love life and see good days*, let him refrain his tongue from evil, and his lips that they may speak no guile: let him eschew evil and do good; let him seek peace, and ensue it.

Yet is that the *whole* of Christianity? Alongside the common language of the 'good', of the pursuit of good days, of the recommendation of the good man and the good woman, lies an *un*common language and an *extra*ordinary vocabulary of redemption. We need something else beyond prudence, and rightly ordered affections. Christianity is about being 'wise unto salvation'. What can that be?

If I had to put that in a shorthand I would say that salvation is found in the dying to live and the falling to rise again. It is what Donald Davie has called the oxymoron of Christianity. Whoever seeks his own loses it; whoever expends himself finds a store, brimming over and pressed down with goodness. This expenditure of self and dying to self-concern is simply the relationship of the gift. If you like, this gift relationship can be rephrased as the highest form of Christian charity and courtesy.

Christ's own birth and death are equally expressions of a charity and a courtesy which we recognize as God's free offering of himself, his movement towards us, his continual seeking of our welfare. We are all already in receipt of infinite charity and treated with unfailing courtesy.

There is even something more at the heart which I find very difficult to put succinctly. It goes like this. This large and humane charity which God offers us in Christ and we are to offer each other in life and in worship (since what is worship but enacted charity?) has its rules and admonitions and disciplines. It has an accumulated wisdom, a holy sensitivity, and applied common sense. But right at the very kernel it drops the appeal to the rule and to lawfulness and asks only for faith, trust and desire. Have you failed? Are you more broken than whole? Are you almost entirely consumed with self? Do you mostly seek your own? Are you eaten into, and away, with guilt or resentment? Are you then almost completely *unexposed*? Well, then, the divine charity remains there undeterred since Christ of his infinite courtesy remains exposed for you and for your salvation. You are still covered and included, and 'the invitation still stands'. The covering note has not been revoked. Just accept and you will know beyond all shadow of doubt that you have already been accepted. 'For I, even I, am he that blotteth out thy transgressions.'

Holy Hospitality

Come unto me all ye that travail and are heavy laden and I will refresh you.
St. Matthew's Gospel, chapter 11, verse 28
(Holy Communion, *Book of Common Prayer*).

I want to think generally of Christianity as a kind of movement of spirit, manifested above all in the *pattern* of the Eucharist, and as certain fundamental *gestures* which punctuate and define that pattern: gestures of invitation and of obeisance, of benediction and charity, of exchange between divine and human, of giving and forgiving, of breakage, unification and exaltation. Christianity is pattern and gestures. How do we enter into that pattern? How do we encounter those gestures?

As we come into church we cross a threshold and set aside momentarily the mundane concerns of our everyday existence. A church is a kind of marker indicating a shift from the chaotic distractions of ordinary busy-ness towards an order and patterning. Our contingent concerns drop away as we begin to align ourselves with that order and allow the pattern to take its hold. We sense that we have been located and placed: not so much by our own will as by a gentle constraint acting upon us.

It is at that point we recognize that we are not so much calling on the house of God, as being called. We are subject to an intimation. That intimation is both a heightening and a loosening. It is a heightening because we are here to pay a particular kind of attention and undergo the rigours of a particular kind of examination. It is a loosening because nothing more is really required of us but an act of alignment. We are present to allow ourselves to be. To be prayerful and worshipful is to be receptive and responsive. The doors of our consciousness, slammed tight by detailed demands and insistent pressures, begin slowly to open.

That means that we are welcomed and welcoming. Think of the deeper meaning of welcome. You are well-come. And nobody asks for your credentials. Nothing further is necessary than your sense that it is good to be here. You are accepted and offered salutations: 'The Lord be with you.' You are drawn into a conversation: 'And with thy spirit.' These are the courtesies which belong to this special kind of house. 'Let us give thanks unto the Lord our God'. 'It is meet and right so to do.'

In this house those whose business it is have already gone about their preparations. The food and drink are already prepared; the cloths are laid; the lights are lit. This is God's board at which you are perfectly free to sit and eat. So this is a form of hospitality, familiar, kindly, domestic.

And yet we are not to be entirely at our ease. We know those things 'whereof our consciences are afraid'. We are certainly familiar, but also alien. Inside each of us there is a secret knowledge of estrangement. At some point we have undergone dislocation, distance, distemper, disease. We know ourselves still inhabitants of a far country who need to be fetched home. And so we do *not* presume. And we need the gestures of cancellation and forgiveness. It is not that God has kept His distance from us, but we have been at a distance from Him. We need comfortable words of all kinds: assurances, absolutions, releases and permissions. Once those comfortable words are pronounced we are fully secure in a spiritual kinship, confident, capable of communion, ready for the movement of God to us-ward.

The key movement in the pattern of Christianity is the proffer of a gift and the realization of a presence. The essential act in redemptive drama is the placing of the gift in our hands. The host offers what has cost him not less than everything: Himself. This is the overflow of the divine generosity: wine as at the wedding in Cana, bread as at the feeding of the five thousand. He is broken and divided to make us whole and to be reconciled with Him: *His* death and *our* transfiguration. For us there is mending in this breaking. It is that brokenness on our account which brings out our own response and engenders the giving of our selves.

What happens then is an exchange of presents between divine host and human guests. To be drawn into the movement from estrangement and forgiveness and into the pattern of the reconciling gift is also to recognize a real presence. We encounter a prior authority. We acknowledge an intimation of sources and destinations altogether outside our range, surpassing the sayable, outside the grasp of what may be dissected and analysed. We are here in a luminous neighbourhood, close to the crossing point on the border between temporal and eternal. We are shifting across the shadow line into the presence of the Most High.

This is not to say that these things always or even often invade our consciousness. We are creatures of anxiety and distraction, subject to brute materiality and the fear of annihilation. It is to say that the pattern of the Eucharist is constantly repeated.

The hospitality is always prepared, the tables ready to be spread, the host is always present, the gifts are always available, and the grace is all sufficient.

Holy Ground and Violation

> Take off thy shoes from off thy feet for the place whereon thou standest is holy ground.
>
> Exodus, chapter 3, verse 5.

> I, if I be lifted up from the earth will draw all men unto me.
>
> St John's Gospel, chapter 12, verse 32.

There are many kinds of holy ground. When Israeli troops captured Jerusalem they went straight to the Wailing Wall and when the French re-entered Paris in 1944 De Gaulle went immediately to Notre Dame. The shrine of the Black Madonna, high in the mountains above Barcelona, is the sacred heart of Catalonia and you approach with care. On medieval maps Jerusalem is represented as the sacred heart of the whole world. So this means that there is one kind of geography that shows you where things are, and another we might call sacred geography, which speaks of what is most precious and significant for a people or a faith. A map may have a physical axis or a spiritual one. A spiritual map for the ancient Greeks would have taken its bearings from the cleft in the rock on the mountains at Delphi and from the Castalian spring. The Greeks and Romans separated sacred from profane and expected profane people to approach with circumspection or keep their distance. The sacred emits a charge which can be very dangerous: think of the dizzying pyramids of sacrifice in Central America or the imperturbable images of crushing power by the Nile at Luxor or the cryptic configurations of sacred landscape between Stonehenge and Avebury.

Today we are less in awe, mixing our reverence with curiosity, and our pilgrimage with tourism. When my wife and I climbed Mount Sinai very early on a Christmas morning our motives combined the revelations of nature and of grace, a rising sun and a spiritual birth. We caught both when she quoted, 'How brightly shines the morning star', and we felt 'it is good for us to be here'.

Contemporary pilgrimage has lost some of its ancient solidarity of faith and people to more personal, more individual feelings of respect. We have partly shifted our holy ground. Walking in an art gallery with a friend we stood in front of a Titian, and he said, half-jokingly, 'Should we kneel?' Walking in Central Park, New York, with our second son, it was for him a pilgrimage to John Lennon's memorial, inscribed with the single word 'Imagine'.

Yet those ancient solidarities and the shared Biblical story are still there as our common resource, especially when life and liberty are at stake. In Memphis, Tennessee there is a memorial to Martin Luther King, murdered there in 1968. It reads 'Behold, this dreamer cometh … come now therefore, and let us slay him … and we shall see what will become of his dreams.' That identifies King as Joseph but in his own last address in Memphis King looked back to Moses. 'I don't know what will happen to me now … Because I've been to the mountain top … I may not get to the promised land with you, but I want you to know tonight that we as a people will.'

There are several overlapping circles of meaning in these very different examples: apartness and demarcation, separating out what matters most from what is indifferent, the sacrifice or untimely death of the bearer of a message, an act of obeisance or gesture of respect, and maybe a change in the self because of an encounter with what is 'Other' or 'not-self'. We are inwardly marked by the power of the sacred marker; and that may happen at the heart of the city or in the solitary place of wilderness or of mountain.

Most of these elements are present when Moses encounters God on Mount Horeb. Once the wandering shepherd has seen the burning bush he is marked out as the reluctant prophet of his people's life and liberty. He makes a gesture of respect and hears the voice of the covenant God of a chosen people set apart for a purpose: 'The God of Abraham, Isaac and Jacob'. He also hears the voice of an unimaginable God whose name is 'I bring to be' or 'I am' or 'I will be what I will be'. He has met the summit of being itself, the creative ground of all that is. This will be the God of the empty space without image or occupant or pronounceable name in the holy of holies at the heart of the temple.

Moses was three times on the holy mountain: for the revelation of a name, for the revelation of a law, and for a distant sight of a land which had been promised but he would not enter. Elijah too came to the same mountain, because he believed the message given him to the people had been rejected. He journeyed forty days and nights through the wilderness, fortified by angelic food and drink, until he stood before the Lord. Then as God the Lord passed by he discovered God was not in the fire, the wind or the earthquake, but in a still, small voice. And he 'wrapped his face in his mantle' before returning renewed to the dangerous city.

Jesus also makes this journey to the solitary place, and more than once: the forty days and nights in the wilderness ministered to by angels; the ascent to the Mount where his face and clothes radiated the glory of God. There the two messengers of the Law and the Prophets, Moses and Elijah, stood beside the Son of Man, before he too set his face to make his own journey to the dangerous city.

The sacred history of the spirit moves backwards and forwards between the solitary place and the city, between the moment of enlightenment and the crisis of confrontation. The holy is not only stillness and light but death and darkness, which is why Jesus, when he urgently asks his disciples to walk in the light (as in John), does so already foreseeing the onset of darkness and death.

We can measure the real presence of the holy by the sense of violation. When Pompey, the Roman conqueror of Jerusalem in 63 BC, entered the empty space of the holy of holies with his soldiers, he committed a gross violation. In our contemporary world we recognize the sacred whenever we hear the language of violation and devastation. The rape and murder of the innocent or the casual evisceration of the bodies of children is desecration. That is why the heart of faith is not only the moment of light and exaltation but the stripping of the body, when the God before whom even the angels veil their faces, is exposed to everything inhuman profanity can devise.

'He gave his back to the smiters, and his cheek to them that plucked out the hair.'

'And there was darkness over all the land from the sixth to the ninth hour, and the veil of the temple was rent from the top unto the bottom.'

Enshrining

> The word of the Lord by Haggai the prophet unto Zerubbabel, governor of Judah … and Joshua the high priest … Is it a time for you, O ye, to dwell in your cieled houses, and this house lie waste?
>
> Haggai, chapter 1, verses 1 and 4.

It is easy to translate the message of the prophet Haggai to refer to our own situation. People then, as now, were more interested in decorating their own houses than with rebuilding the House of God. A cieled house was one luxuriously ornamented with timber. So the Temple and all it stood for lay neglected, and alongside that neglect went a deep dissatisfaction. The wage earner, says Haggai, put his wages into a bag of holes. People drank, yet their deeper thirsts were unslaked; they ate yet felt a deeper hunger. The state of the Temple reflected the condition of their hearts.

In 1934, T.S. Eliot wrote a short verse play which was really a commentary on this prophetic message:

> The world turns and the world changes,
> But one thing does not change.
> In all my years, one thing does not change.
> However you disguise it, this thing does not change.
> The perpetual struggle of Good and Evil.
> Forgetful, you neglect your shrines and churches …
>
> (*The Rock*)

A lot has changed since 1934 and a lot more since 520 BC, but this thing does not change: the neglect of the shrine and what it stands for. There are, after all, more immediate concerns: the car, the office, the house, the children.

In any case, there are those who believe that the struggle of Good and Evil has little to do with the care of the shrine and the state of the Temple. People can be good without tending or attending the shrine; and in the real world out there the operative houses belong to merchant bankers and industrial researchers, not to God. You can cite religious tradition itself for the view that God does not dwell in houses made with hands, but universally in creation and the human heart. The temple is a mere external form just as the pattern of worship is a mere external form, and consecration is just a form of words. The sacred has no location, but resides only in the values and aspirations we hold most dear. One place cannot be holier than another. So they say.

All that is almost true, yet it is not a whole truth. A shrine marks something, and how we treat it and approach it tells us something. When our own house was gutted by fire while we were abroad, our children rang to say the Bible and the photos were safe. Those things were *not* the family yet they were the visible icons of our little lot, and part of what was most precious resided in them. So, too, the divine resides in part in its icons, and our sense of communal worth resides in what we set aside and elevate as holy or precious. Throughout most of human history people have set aside and elevated that which is both holy to God and most precious to themselves. When London burned it mattered that St Paul's stood, because concentrated there was all that belonged to us of continuity, seriousness and aspiration, and all that belonged to the holy. The shrine of the Most High continued to stand on the high ground. Place earths the sacred. A church, any church, is 'a serious place on serious earth'.

What I am trying to say is that the inwardness of the spirit manifests itself in visible signs, and that there is no community so bereft of spirit that it fails to create some outward sign of transcendent meaning and faith. We need to be able to visualize and handle what we are about, and to create a space or edifice or shrine where to read, mark, and learn, what ultimately matters. The human city is not just the sprawling intersection of business interests or the concentration of political powers. If it were the expression of business interests then London might well be represented by the National Westminster Bank. It is twice as high as St Paul's. Yet everybody knows it is only a fragment of what we are and what we intend. We do not envisage the continuity of our city through the National Westminster Bank, and we do not read there the spiritual genealogy of our civilization. You do not visit a bank to recollect or aspire, to hope, to embrace charity, to mourn, to celebrate, to make music or to meditate.

And if business cannot focus our common life nor can politics. What happened in eastern Europe in the course of 1989 said something about where the spiritual genealogy of a civilization can be found. We have not yet absorbed the magnitude of what happened to all of us in 1989. We now know the spiritual genealogy of our civilization cannot be relocated in party headquarters. When the spirit of all the peoples of the East began to move it visited churches and carried candles. The Communist Party headquarters in East Germany aimed to be the soul of a people and now it is dead, a monument to the failure of dialectical materialism. The ancient guardians of the spirit remain, still neglected, but still there. Power is not an ultimate any more than money is an ultimate. The sacred heart of a society cannot in the last resort be the ruling powers of the polis, or the Deutschmark and pound sterling.

So what is a shrine? A shrine has to be an island of quietness in which to recite the narratives of our redemption and our recovery. Here we tell the redemptive story; the tale of the loving purposes of God. A shrine has to to with our wholeness and our common concern. So it can be used to protest against blemishes on our corporate life and also to recollect the honour of the nation. A shrine gives sanctuary to the refugee and hosts a national celebration. And it is inclusive because whoever enters does so solely on account of being human. The vast doorways of cathedrals offer an inclusive human embrace. The first and only requirement of entry is desire to enter. You enter a bank as a depositor, a town hall as a politician, but you enter the domain of the holy as a living soul. A shrine is a template – temple and template are identical words – cut out of the ordinary world to make a difference and signify that other things are possible and potent; churches are beautiful, more beautiful even than palaces, precisely because they are ways of colonizing earth on behalf of heaven. The colony provides an orientation pointing eastwards to the source of true light and upwards to infinity.

A shrine is not only a template of the perfect but the space in which we say and enact what is most basic to human living. What goes on here is a word and a gesture of gift and reception, offering and thanksgiving. Gifts are passed from hand to hand with all the attendant courtesies of obeisance and blessing. The gift and the shared table are at the sacred heart of any serious human existence and they find their expression and solemn enactment in the high and holy place.

So the state of the shrine and the condition of the temple is not a matter of the care of ancient buildings and conservation areas. It has to do with a colony of the other Kingdom, with the only space dedicated solely to contrition and aspiration, and the enactment of justice and charity. The word of Haggai to Zerubbabel, governor of Judah, and to Joshua, the high priest, is therefore a word to us:

> Is it a time for you, O ye, to dwell in your cieled houses, and this house lie waste?

Denying the Temple?

The Most High dwelleth not in temples made with hands.

Book of the Acts, chapter 7, verse 48.

This text sounds harmless enough, but we find it towards the conclusion of the last speech of Christianity's first martyr. It is part of a bitter debate about the Temple and about the Law, going back to Christ himself. Of course, both sides were appealing to the same Scripture, but the texts had different meanings and in Acts we overhear the echoes of increasing conflict. Christians selected themes from Israel's repertory of faith and began to transpose them more and more radically until there emerged something called Christianity, and eventually something we now call Judaism.

It is the way of revolutions to begin slowly in a shift of emphasis and a change of accent. Our own English Revolution in the 1640s was a century in the making and partly began in matters such as what you wear and do in church. Though Jesus addressed Jews as a Jew, the long-term implications of his change of accent were enormous, and as the conflict grew these implications were drawn out with revolutionary consequences still with us today. We think we live in a post-Christian society, which we do, but how we understand, think and feel feeds off roots deep in the New Testament – and also (and this is important) of necessity in the Old.

Let me ask you for a moment to put aside Christianity as a creed, and instead think of it as an approach and as a revolutionary vision which could turn the world upside down in a couple of sentences. For example: 'Consider the lilies of the field how they grow ... I tell you Solomon in all his glory was not arrayed like one of these.' So the 'meanest flower that blows' (to quote Wordsworth) is more beautiful than Solomon, the founder of the Temple. I have no idea how the ancient world looked at lilies but these two sentences, expressing gratitude for the miracle of growth in nature, make up one of those tiny seeds of revolution which one day themselves grow miraculously till they encompass everything we see.

When Jesus placed a child at the centre of the group of his friends, and made childhood a sign of the kingdom he dropped another seed that took nearly eighteen hundred years to grow. Again, when the temple guard arrived with swords and staves, he told his friends, 'Put up your sword' because he knew the kingdom could not 'come by violence'. At that moment the heavens – mentally – 'parted from pole to pole', and every regime of violence was thrown into doubt. So then, in about six sentences all told, we are invited to see the sword, the child and the lily in a new light; and these changes in our angle of vision are not so much new beliefs as enlightenments.

I could give many more examples of radical changes in the angle of vision. There is the identification of the Almighty God in the broken body of a suffering man, the reversal of status in the kingdom or the saying, 'He that humbles himself shall be exalted'. That single sentence actually provides the fundamental pattern of the creed itself: 'He that descended is also He that ascended.'

But our particular text is about the Temple and the Law, so how have Christians turned upside down the worlds of the Temple and the Law? The answer is by a shift of accent. Though Jesus came to 'fulfil the Law' he also taught that defilement came from within us not from without, and that the Sabbath was made for man not man for the Sabbath. If we translate that it means that the Law, which is our necessary frame of action, is also an instrument for human flourishing. Our obedience to it includes purity of heart and intention as well as our outward and visible actions. Translate that again and we find that we stand directly before God not the tribunal of the tribe, justified not by the works of the Law but by grace and faith. We have been made witnesses to conscience and truth, though it may cost us excommunication, or in Stephen's case, life itself.

The issue of the Temple is the question of the Law put another way, if we consider what the Temple means. The holy place at the centre of the city anchors your birthright membership in the house of Israel, its Law and its land. In that holy place you receive the indelible birth mark of circumcision and are made a member of Israel according to the Law. But now, according to these Christians, the local temple has been turned into the universal body of Christ and membership in that body through baptism is not by birth but by choice and grace. For Christians the history of Israel is as much one of dispersion as of settlement and they have given up the hope of 'next year in Jerusalem' to become universal citizens in a heavenly Zion. The physical temple is now an allegory of the spiritual building within ourselves, our souls and bodies, and we discover it when we come together as the friends of God in the body of Christ.

We have been conducting a kind of thought experiment to imagine once more the tension between the early church and the Jews, indeed the world, which happens also to be the tension between grace and our nature. Christianity threatened not only the tribe and the holy place in the holy land, but the family too. That above all is difficult to imagine because we have not had many sermons lately on becoming a eunuch for the sake of the kingdom or on the grace of perpetual virginity.

Here I return to what I suggested earlier about needing the Old Testament as well as the New, because it lowers this tension between grace and nature. It is our natural associations in family and tribe which give us location, identity, purpose and meaning, and offer us a story in which to play a part. We all require the bearings provided by the Law, the markers and boundaries that confer belonging, and continuities which pass from one generation to another. We need temples at the heart of our common life to house what we hold most holy.

So have we then been forced to abandon the New Testament because humanly we are embedded in family, people, land and holy place? Not at all. Rather we discover what it is to possess dual citizenship in the City of Man and the City of God. We exploit and endure a creative ambiguity between the ties of nature and the call of grace, the demands of the Law and the scrutiny of conscience, the commemorations of the tribe and the perpetual memorial and anticipation of universal redemption. We are glad to enter within the gates of the temple 'whither the tribes go up', knowing nevertheless that God is not confined 'in temples made with hands' but takes up his abode with the pure in heart, made known anywhere two or three are gathered together in His name.

Vision and Intimation

The days are at hand and the effect of every vision.

Ezekiel, chapter 12, verse 23.

(Or as The Revised English Bible has it 'The days are near when every vision will be fulfilled'.)

I want to look at 'vision': visions of the world, visions of human society, visions of human life and humankind. The exact context in which Ezekiel uttered these words does not matter very much for my purpose, except to say that Ezekiel was composing a kind of political and religious journal in the early years of the sixth century BC. It was a time when many Jews were in exile but others were still in their homeland. Ezekiel foresaw the fall of Jerusalem as the sacred centre of the Jewish world and set himself to denounce false prophets and diviners, particularly those who claimed that vision had failed and that the revelation of God was now indefinitely postponed. On the contrary, said Ezekiel, the vision is very close and you will know very soon that God is the Lord. Ezekiel himself was the bearer of the vision; the spirit God would breathe into the dry bones.

Out of that vision has sprung much of our visionary literature, especially Milton and Blake. We live still in that visionary light, even if we haven't read *Paradise Lost* or Blake's prophetic books. Of course, we take that vision out of its local base in the history of Israel and apply it to ourselves. The moment the Promenaders at the Albert Hall sing 'Jerusalem' they are engulfed in that vision as it touches on our time and our place. Will God's will be done and His Kingdom come here on this earth, in this realm, in this England? Wider than that, will the knowledge of God cover the whole earth as the waters cover the sea? What does the vision of God mean for our fragile and precarious world? Is it a diminishing archaic whimper, half-remembered, or a pregnant hint and intimation of things that shall be?

Let me for a moment invoke the vision, so that we recollect its power. Listen to John Milton as he refashions Ezekiel for his time and his place.

The Lord will come, and *not be slow*;
His footsteps cannot err;
Before Him righteousness shall go,
His royal harbinger.

Truth from the earth, like to a flower,
Shall bud and blossom then;
And justice, from her heavenly bower
Look down on mortal men.

Rise, Lord, judge Thou the earth in might,
This longing earth redress;

For thou art He who shall by right
The nations all possess.

The moment is imminent; the promise is not prolonged; the chariots of fire are prepared and the arrows of desire poised, the clouds ready to unfold – with what Ezekiel calls 'Glory'.

But, when all is said and sung, what can these intimations of glory possibly mean? We can, of course, imagine them, through poetry and music. What looks like wistful wish fulfilment becomes through imagery and musical sounds potently present. Through poetry and music we recognize that this vision awakens a correspondence in ourselves. Whenever we are tempted to view ourselves as mundanely enclosed, constricted, diminished, half-dead, trapped in the everyday, there is this returning presence, full of intimation and immediate promise. We sense that we are on the edge of something waiting to break through. And that is where faith's heart lies: in the sense of what waits to break through. It waits; and it breaks. It lies there all the time; and yet (like the world) it moves all the same. God's Kingdom is not postponed to some future 'far-off divine event' but lies on the edge of the present.

When it comes to the understanding and the realization of this vision there are two equal and opposite dangers. One is the danger of locating the kingdom as *here* and *there*: the falsehood of premature identification. This danger is greatest when any nation or party identifies itself as the embodiment of promise. A political party or a nation seeing itself as a secular realization of God's kingdom on earth proclaims an omnipotence and omniscience it cannot possibly have, and is a harbinger of repression and violence. The kingdom of God does not come by violence, but by love's sacrificial intervention.

The other danger is forgetfulness of promise, and immersion in the everyday. When that happens everything that *is* appears indefinitely prolonged. Material wants and satisfactions set the limit on desire and cut off the horizon of hope. People cease to hear any more this prophetic warning that God remains God and that the demands of righteousness and justice are not set aside. 'Where there is no vision the people perish', because the scales of judgement, of our priorities and what we value, and of what we set forward as the true and chief end of humankind, are tipped in the wrong direction.

In all this the church exists to be the still small voice of vision heard below the cacophony of contemporary demands. However immersed it may be in its own version of the mundane; the Church carries forward a persistent and prophetic reminder of a proper ordering of human lives and the affairs of nations. If that seems very unlikely remember that there is no other association of humans existing solely to mourn our losses, reclaim our hopes, and affirm the intimation of the Kingdom of righteousness and peace. Where else if not here? When else if not now?

Peace and Unity

> For he is our peace who has made us both one, and has broken down the dividing wall of hostility, by abolishing in his flesh the law of commandments and ordinances, that he might create in himself one new man, instead of the two, so making peace.
>
> St Paul's Letter to the Ephesians, chapter 2, verses 14–15 (*RSV*).

> (A sub-text from the Koran: 'I have made you, O mankind, male and female, that you may know each other and not dwell in tribes.')

The key phrases in this text are about breaking down the dividing wall, and about the creation of an undivided humanity in Christ.

In the context of Ephesians as a whole this is Christianity's breakthrough to the idea of a unified mankind under one God. It is a charter of universal inclusion and also a declaration of independence from Jewish origins. Of course, much, perhaps most, had been already foreshadowed in the Jewish exploration into God, but the breakthrough accomplished here is final and unmistakeable, setting aside the special law, and circumcision as the marker of inherent difference. Jesus was not just a Jewish Messiah fulfilling the hope of Israel but the universal redeemer of our human race.

The immediate surrounds of this text rest on a few key images, the body – as Christ and as the Church, the building, especially the Temple, cross-referenced against the body – and also the corner stone. But first we ought to look at its political imagery. Listen to this. The distant stranger and the alien have been included as fellow citizens of the commonwealth. It sounds very modern. And it is, because though the context is faith, you can – as so often in the New Testament – overhear future translations in political terms. With only a shift of phraseology the idea of a single humanity under 'God the Father of all' becomes another and more recent Declaration of Independence. 'We hold these truths to be self-evident that all men are created equal, that they are endowed by their Creator with certain unalienable rights … life, liberty and the pursuit of Happiness.' In the same way Paul's 'glorious liberty' of the sons of God trembles on the edge of political translation. Imagine how a slave in the Caribbean or the Deep South might hear the words 'You are no longer slaves but sons … and if sons then heirs, joint-heirs with Christ'.

Of course, early Christians could not and did not follow through on this imagery of the commonwealth and the common family. They were themselves divided over just this issue. As Christianity expanded many Christians became assimilated to Roman ideas of a distinction between civilized and barbarian; and they accepted slavery, just as many of those who proclaimed equality in the American Declaration of Independence accepted it. But ticking away underneath was this subversive vocabulary of Paul – and the story of Jesus – waiting to explode in the face of established Christianity itself. If in Christ there is neither male nor female, Jew nor Greek, bond nor free, what does that imply for all the Christian debates about whether native Americans were human, and all the other dividing lines of human history, up to apartheid and the Berlin Wall? Paul's meaning is clear, that although there is variety and difference, what unites overrides what separates. The wall is down.

We could then treat this dense impacted text in Ephesians as a hymn to unity. As such it looks back as well as forward, above all (like the Koran) to the story of Creation. The idea of the generic is rooted in Genesis, because it was *one* God that made the heaven and the earth and created Man, female and male, in the undivided divine image. The creed is another hymn to unity: I believe in one God, one Lord, one baptism. And the very first chapter of Ephesians brings out how the one is related to the all. The God and Father of 'our Lord Jesus Christ' is a fullness waiting and seeking to 'fill all in all'.

But what of the other images in this passage, the body, the building, the temple and the breaking down of the barrier of special status, including particular laws? Paul is referring to the partition in the temple which divided the outer court of the Gentiles from the inner court of the Jews and he is saying that in Christ, the Federal Head of our kind, there is now a single space and a common concourse. The physical temple of stone, with the physical Jerusalem, has been translated into a sign of the one universal spirit with shared access to the Father, making peace where once there was hostility and separation.

This is, of course, a visionary anticipation of a condition which far transcends the fractured and rivalrous enmities of contemporary humanity, only too clearly illustrated in Jerusalem itself. But we need to go beyond even this vision to a profound level where the text deals with love, death and what Paul calls justification, that is the free cancellation of our indebtedness before the law. The sublime argument of Ephesians on these fundamentals has to be taken in two brief stages, each focussed on the body of Christ, first as the Church, then as the frail body driven out of the city and impaled at Golgotha.

First, as to the Church, viewed as the spiritual body and living temple of those incorporated in Christ, we miss its extraordinary character as depicted here, on account of familiarity and the inevitable brokenness of all human institutions. Yet this is the body which carries forward in its foundation documents the idea of a global community transcending all the natural memberships of family and tribe. It bears the imprint of the City of God. However pock-marked and Balkanized by fragmentation the Church projects the vision of a cross-border institution of brothers and sisters who freely choose an adoption by the Baptism of the Spirit. It entertains, willy nilly, the hope of a common concourse and a single space.

But deeper and deeper still, as to love, death and the forgiveness of our debts before the law of God, Ephesians recognises the deadly *cost* of the fracture in ourselves and of a humanity divided into citizen and alien. Such was the cost that the temple of Christ's body was destroyed in a holocaust of enmity, before it was raised again 'in the heavenly places'. Yet Christ by emptying himself of all but love overcame enmity itself, leading captivity captive. The one whom Jerusalem, the archetypal City of Man, despised, rejected and threw outside the wall, converted disgrace to grace, the death-dealing to the life-giving. By making the vehicles of violence the instruments of love he became our Peace. So *now* we can put the last image into place: the stone which the builders rejected has become the coping stone, the foundation, of the living temple of the holy spirit of the one God.

Murder and Blood Brotherhood

See now there comes a reckoning for [Joseph's] blood.
Genesis, chapter 42, verse 22.

The cup of blessing which we bless is it not a sharing in the blood of Christ?
St. Paul, First Epistle to the Corinthians, chapter 10, verse 16.

You cannot partake of the table of the Lord and the table of demons.
St. Paul, First Epistle to the Corinthians, chapter 10, verse 21.

I want to think about three murder stories. I ask you to keep in mind the themes of blood, brotherhood and 'he who would be greatest'. These themes are very obvious in my first story, of Joseph and his envious brethren, because the cue for murder begins with Joseph's dream of outshining all the rest. So his brothers, perhaps understandably in view of his superior coat and superior mother, threw him in a pit, leaving him for dead. But our Wunderkind escaped to become Grand Vizier of Egypt. Then the tables turned because his wise policies meant there was corn in Egypt. His brothers had to leave their famine-stricken land and come to him for sustenance. They did not realize who he was and he accused them of spying and thieving, and made the price of their freedom that they return home and bring with them their father's youngest and best-beloved son. Stunned in their hearts it was Reuben who turned to his brothers and said 'So now there comes a reckoning for Joseph's blood'. Blood shed between those who share the same blood cries out from the ground for justice – just as it did when Cain slew his brother Abel.

The second story is not about blood relations but about a bond between seven partners in murder sealed in the blood of their noble victim. This is a different kind of blood brotherhood. Out of mixed motives of envy, and of peace and liberty in a free republic they feared he planned to make himself ruler over them. The republic is Rome and the noble victim Julius Caesar, and in Shakespeare's play the seven conspirators circle their master before each plunging in the knife.

Then, as a seal of unity, Brutus demands they 'bathe their hands in Caesar's blood'. Each now shares in the betrayal of friendship, and their common guilt binds them in a demonic brotherhood. The blood that was shed cries out for a reckoning and their unity shatters. The law of a life for a life requires that those who take the sword perish by the sword.

As in the second story the third is not about blood relations, though there are once again twelve in the group. They seek a kingdom of peace where the truth shall set them free. But one evening when their little fraternity of love comes together to share meat and drink with their master, one of their number, perhaps hoping to bring about the peaceable kingdom by violence, gives way to the demon inside him. He goes out into the night, only to return with soldiers and betray his lord with a kiss. Jesus is then accused of setting himself up to be king and the mob closes round him crying 'Hail, king of the Jews' and 'We have no king but Caesar'. So the shared bread and wine of that final supper become the body broken and the blood shed, for us and for many on Calvary.

These are all famous stories and the third is the story of stories. They are strangely similar while being profoundly different, because *the meaning of blood differs* as does the nature of the bond of blood, and the working out of a deep fracture in human relations.

In the story of Joseph matters are fairly simple; indeed, it is less tragic, less fundamental than the story of Cain and Abel. The murder in the brothers' hearts is only attempted, and the family is reunited by the generous forgiveness of the intended victim. In the story of Julius Caesar a deadly dynamic of peace and freedom sought by violence sets off the rough justice of a life for a life, and more. The republic is divided and lost. In the story of the Passion, injustice and violence are met by forgiveness, and Christ by his offering of himself makes of one blood all the nations upon earth. The kingdom is won.

But how? We have to look deeper into the differences. The one who would be greatest in the Kingdom of God is so only because he is the servant of all, and we are not talking about the natural family based on blood, or the political kingdom resting on blood and violence, but about a kingdom not of this world. The brothers and sisters of the spiritual family share a common citizenship in the Father's kingdom. In the republic lost, evil is paid back; in the kingdom won, love is poured out. It is a life for a life in both, but the blood given reverses the blood taken. For the holy one who gave his blood the cup was bitter and could not be taken away; for us who receive and share that blood the cup 'runneth over'.

As Brutus looked at the handiwork of the conspirators he, and perhaps they too, imagined a future of peace and liberty, where this exemplary tyrannicide would be continually re-enacted in tongues unknown and countries unborn. He did not yet know that this was an altar of demons from which no good or peace could come. In this fallen world the blood sacrifice and the betrayal of friendship only exact more blood.

What Christ imagined was a coming together of all the children of God to sit down in companies and share the common table, and that has indeed borne fruits in truth and love. But again, in this world of sin, with its wars and rumours of wars, where some kind of peace *is* sometimes brought by justified violence, there are no easy and assured alleluias, not even in music. The antithesis of political 'republic lost' and Spiritual 'Kingdom won' is not so easy. Augustine tried to establish a community of peace, truth and mutual love, as did Gregory, Benedict and Francis, yet – in Paul's words – they found there is always a 'table of demons' somewhere in the paradise garden. Our perfect and sufficient redemption turns then, on hope and faith not sight. Yet whenever we come together in companies at the table, its offering of meat and drink is a foretaste of the kingdom. And he took the cup and gave thanks and gave it to them saying 'Drink ye all of it; for this is my blood of the new testament, which is shed for you and for many for the remission of sins. But I say unto you: I will not drink henceforth from the fruit of the vine, until that day when I drink it new with you in my Father's kingdom'.

Angelic and Demonic[1]

> What is man that thou art mindful of him … ? [yet] thou hast made him a little lower than the angels.
>
> Psalm 8, verses 4 and 5.

My theme is angels, but I must begin with the demonic as well as the angelic because they belong together. If no demons, no angels; no angels, no demons. I argue evident hell is linked to evident heaven.

From the New Testament to *The Dream of Gerontius* angels and demons are parts of the same celestial and infernal cast. According to Richard Hooker the fallen angels were prideful delinquents trooping across the stage to re-emerge as idols, demons and infernal deities.

In any case the idea of soaring and resplendent being, rational and concordant, has to have its mirror in bizarre, gross and malign possession. And our own experience agrees, because we all have inklings of involuntary perfection, say Mozart in the act of composition, and of acts of inhumanity beyond all conscience and comprehension.

Perhaps the angelic and the demonic mark the upper and the lower limits of a scale where ordinary humans play the middle range. To be human is to occupy an ambiguous middle state; so an enquiry into angels and demons is an enquiry into ourselves. We need them to think with. If we follow Augustine in supposing them personifications of presences and powers then they can be our guides to the grandeur and the misery of man. (And were there time, we might use today's fascination with the threatening powers and presences of 'aliens' to enquire into a related ambiguity of our modern condition: our scientific freedom to manipulate the environment and the scientific reduction of humanity to genetic programming with no inner freedom at all.)

But some will say: let us at least be clear that angels and demons belong to those times of ignorance when humanity imagined itself exposed to benign and malign enchantments. Well, of course, we know we are not talking about wings and horns, and it is also true that so far as scientific psychology goes angelic presence of mind and the chaos of possession are equally invisible. But then for a science, any science, so self-limited by its own purposes, the infinite spaces of our own minds are just as invisible as angels. And what psychology is it that deals in courage, faith and hope, in joy and love, which we cannot doubt at the heart of everything?

The moment we ourselves directly encounter degradation and devastation we go back, not just to the language of good and evil, but to bedevilment and possession. Who has never encountered an open season in hell; and after such knowledge who is exempt from the need for exorcism, let alone the need for forgiveness? There are hauntings and infestations whose name is legion which require those healing presences and protecting powers. From Hieronymus Bosch to Francis Bacon and Beckmann the demonic is before our very eyes, especially maybe since the First World War, though I do not know where today we might unlock the restoratives.

Enough of hell because my argument is that evident hell implies evident heaven. An ambiguous being haunted by death and hell's destruction is also haunted by perfection. The persistent rumour of angels is not a throwback to antique enchantments but a testament of immortal longings. Angels 'ever bright and fair' are there ready to lead us into garden cities of paradise. Why else are we so rapt by '*In paradisum deducant angeli ... Jerusalem, Jerusalem*' or by the mighty Sabbaths of Peter Abelard: '*O quanta qualia sunt illa Sabbata?*' The words angel and evangel both mean to bear a divine word, so perhaps we can best enquire into angels by asking just where in sacred scripture they make their entrances.

Angels bring good tidings to Mary and the benighted shepherds; they greet women hurrying at first light to an empty tomb. They are ministers of grace in the wilderness of temptation and the Garden of the Agony; they bring light and liberty to Peter in prison. They announce the dissolution and restoration of worlds that are passing away and are jubilant presences at the Supper of the Lamb.

Yet it is here, just here, we uncover the limits of perfection and how it is we humans are crowned with glory and honour. I take my first cue from George Herbert in his hymn

> To all Angels and Saints:
> Oh glorious spirits who after all your bands
> See the smooth face of God without a frown,
> or strict commands ...

So angels, having no access to time, know nothing of law or freedom, transgression or judgement, or reprieve. Unfallen innocence can never know grace. As the liturgy for Easter Eve has it: 'O blessed sin that brought so great redemption.'

I take my second cue from Richard Hooker who says that angels, though self-contained, *need* our society and fellowship. (James Macmillan's oratorio *Parthenogenesis* explores that same theme by reflection on a documented case of spontaneous cloning where, unlike Gabriel, the angel of that Annunciation is wounded by care for the predicament of an identical mother and daughter.) What Hooker must mean by 'need' is that the angelic symphony lacks movement until the entry of the human voice, and that is because we alone of creatures live in a far country while still remembering home. The forte of the angels is *Gloria*, *Hosanna* and *Sanctus* with trumpets, but they cannot petition for mercy – *Kyrie Eleison*, or sue for peace – *Dona nobis pacem*. It is never their part to sing 'He was crucified also *for us*'. They have never been suddenly awestruck or 'surprised by joy'. These are *our* privileges.

The idea of the angelic is an imagination of perfect intelligences in planetary procession round the eternal source of light. The question their mere intelligences cannot answer is 'Why did God become man?' It is grace abounding, grace alone, and nothing but grace.

William Fuller has a meditation on this (set by Purcell in his *Harmonia Sacra*) which conveys angelic bafflement at the divine secretion in time and the taking of humanity into God.

What is man, lost man, that thou shouldst be
So mindful of him, that the Son of God
Forsook his glory, his abode,
To become a poor, tormented man!
The deity was shrunk into a span
And that for me, O wondrous love, for me …
Blest spirits tell
Which did excel
Which was more prevalent
Your joy or your astonishment?
That man should be assum'd into the deity.
That for a worm a God should'st die? …

In this we see unfolded the meaning of the Christmas epistle 'Unto which of the angels said he at any time "Thou art my son, this day have I begotten thee."' *This* day and *my* son tell us that incarnate love has to be realized in a particular time and place. The particular is no scandal, or rather it is the same scandal as the cross. Only the one who undergoes the space-bound, time-bound journey has the freedom to pursue a true love open to wounding and defeat. Yet what else is there?

'Tis mystery all! the Immortal dies!
Who can explore his strange design?
In vain the first-born seraph tries
To sound the depths of love divine!
'Tis mercy all, let earth adore,
Let angel minds inquire no more!

(Charles Wesley)

Note

1 Patronal Festival, St Michael's, Cornhill.

The Venom and Wisdom of Serpents

> These twelve Jesus sent forth ... to the lost sheep of Israel ... [saying] be ye therefore wise as serpents and harmless as doves.
>
> St Matthew's Gospel, chapter 10, verses 5, 6 and 16.

> Behold, the ark of the covenant ... passeth before you into Jordan ... Now therefore take you twelve men out of the tribes of Israel ...
>
> Joshua, Chapter 3, verses 11 and 12.

This is a sacred entertainment in which I want to arrive eventually at this curious wisdom of the serpent; but I begin at some distance from my texts.

The Bible is above all else a story, and as Christians read it that story runs from the garden of Eden, where paradise was lost, to the garden of Gethsemane and the garden of the Resurrection where paradise began to be regained. In the garden of Eden the loss of paradise really set everything else in motion: work, conflict, sex, shame, conjugal love, birth and fertility – and the twinning of death with life in the creation of future generations. In the gardens of Gethsemane and the Resurrection death is again twinned with life, but this time to secure the *re*-generation of mankind as part of the *re*-creation of the world.

The Bible then has a pattern of reprise with a difference built into its story-line from start to finish. Just when the story starts to repeat itself you find you have turned a different corner. The familiar is also the transformed. Supposing we put together Moses crossing the Red Sea and Joshua crossing the Jordan. This is clearly the same foundation story, simply divided into parts one and two. When Jesus comes to Jordan he and the people know this is a dramatic reprise. This is yet another new beginning and a gesture of inauguration. But the people do not know what new corner has been turned or recognize the arrival of a new spirit. The old Joshua and this new Jeshua will both save their people, but the warlord bent on occupation and ethnic cleansing is very far from the Prince of Peace. Joshua and Jeshua alike pass through a baptism by water, but as Jesus makes his passage through the water it is the holy and harmless dove of peace which settles upon his head.

The tenth chapter of Matthew is yet another and related reprise with a difference: the twelve tribes who seek allotted territory have now become the twelve disciples 'without sword or scrip', who take a message about a kingdom not of this world, first to the people of Israel; and then (at the conclusion of Matthew's Gospel) they offer a universal baptism in the spirit to all nations.

The principle of reprise with a difference not only governs the big story but is echoed in all its images and emblems, above all those to do with the body and its food and drink. So the manna that mysteriously sustains the Israelites in the Wilderness becomes our spiritual food for today in the Lord's Prayer, and the wine that gladdens the heart of man is turned into the gift of the life-blood of Christ.

And, of course, the poetry of Christianity in liturgy and hymnody is simply the recomposition both of events in the story and of emblems drawn from the natural world. As for emblems drawn from the natural world just think how wheat and apples, lambs and lions, fire and water, fish and honeycombs, are recomposed as signs of the resurrection and the life. As for events in the story just think how Christian writers rework Joshua's first crossing of Jordan as our passage through death to life:

'Captain of Israel's host and Guide of all that seek the land above'; 'Part of the host has crossed the flood and part is crossing now'; 'When I tread the verge of Jordan, Bid my anxious fears subside, Death of deaths and hell's destruction, Land me safe on Canaaan's side.' The promised land of Israel has been transformed into the universal spiritual home of humanity.

Let me now conclude with two emblems drawn from the natural world which play one role in *Paradise Lost* and a very different one in *Paradise Regained.* I choose the apple tree and the serpent, which are both deadly in the beginning but life-giving in the action replay. The apple becomes good and the serpent truly wise.

First, as to the fruit of the apple tree it is part of the original creation which Emily Dickinson called 'This Whole Experiment with Green'. Yet its 'fatal taste' precipitated our entry into the knowledge of good and evil and so into a potential rivalry with God, whose image we still bear. But then in the Christian reading of the Song of Songs we once again come upon the secret entrance into the garden of our first true love, at the heart of which stands Christ 'the apple tree'. The fruit of that tree is no longer deadly but in the words of Revelation 'for the healing of the nations'. Another New England poet picks that up by showing how the sight of Christ re-creates that first 'Experiment in Green': 'The tree of life my soul has seen, Laden with fruit and always green, The trees of nature fruitless be, Compared with Christ the apple tree.'

As for the serpent he is a fascinating kettle of fish. He turns up in the original garden as the most subtle of all the beasts of the field, perhaps because he has already been up the tree and enjoyed surreptitious bites of the apple. At any rate he knows how to argue and we might see him as the first philosopher–theologian, slyly questioning the hitherto taken-for-granted. And, of course, he subverts the woman first because she is more apt for new ideas than her stolid helpmeet. In the long run the serpent is doing us all a good turn because without disobedience the story of redemption cannot get going. No loss, no gain. Nevertheless we all know his intervention has a very serious downside of which I mention just two aspects. The first, as Milton makes clear in Book 9 of *Paradise Lost*, is the duplicity of language. The wiliness of the subtle serpent is his command of rhetoric: the defective glory, the miraculous seduction, of persuasive speech. The second aspect is the warfare between the human and the natural: the seed of woman crushes the serpent's head and he bruises his heel. Man and nature go out of tune and we are thrown into creative dischord.

But like the apple the serpent comes back again with a very different character. Once we move on to the Book of Numbers and the Book of Proverbs his wily poison has changed to healing wisdom. When the Israelites in the wilderness are plagued by serpent bites, Moses holds up a brazen serpent which when they look on it provides their healthful antidote. The uplifted emblem of a divine virtue and wisdom is the salve of malignancy and enmity. Now apply this marvellous change. Just as Jesus Christ is the tree for the healing of the nations, who renders good once more God's first 'Experiment in Green', so when we look on Jesus Christ, and him crucified, the potent virtue of his wounds draws out the poisoned malignancy of ours. Jesus, prefiguring his death, embraces that terrible and marvellous emblem: 'As Moses lifted up the serpent in the wilderness, so also must the Son of Man be lifted up.' 'For I, if I be lifted up, will draw all men unto me.' Thanks be to God.

The Family Resemblances of Wisdom

But where shall wisdom be found? and where is the place of understanding?
Book of Job, chapter 28, verse 12.

The 28th chapter of Job is a two-part poem. The first part graphically describes man's rough, tough encounter with the natural world only to say that wisdom lies elsewhere, while the second part finds wisdom in the fear of the Lord. I expect many contemporary Christians may find this contrast rather too sharp. After the Franciscan revolution and after the scientific revolution we feel more inclined to echo the Creation Hymn in Psalm 104, 'O Lord, how manifold are thy works, in wisdom hath thou made them all'. There is, after all, a wisdom wrested from the order of nature by science through what the eighth chapter of Proverbs calls 'weight and measurement'. There is also a 'wise passiveness' as we absorb what Baudelaire called 'the forest of symbols' in the vast temple of nature.

But the writer of Job is not thinking of the wisdom and power that a tool-bearing animal wrests from nature but of the moral experience a sign-giving, word-using animal wrests from life. Our knowledge of nature depends on order, inevitability, and recurrence. Our experience of ourselves arises because we look before and after, free to learn from our retrospective regret and animated by an uncertain prospect, hedged with hope and fear. We are part of a drama, forward-looking and even, to some extent, open-ended, framed by language and a living creative word, not just by impersonal fates or forces.

Job, then, invites us to pursue a wisdom of human existence under divine scrutiny. In that pursuit we encounter mysterious springs of light and life, love and fulfilment, which we try to trace to source. Our guide is not what Pascal called the 'spirit of geometry' with its precise deductions, or even the mystical absorption that registers impulses 'from a vernal wood', but coded sightings, images and emblems coming out of our experience of light and dark, order and chaos, fulfilment and frustration, growth and decay, hope and regret, judgement and reprieve. The Bible is our code book, setting these sightings in great clusters or families of image, metaphor and analogy, and showing how all these genealogies lead back to a common family tree.

My example is, of course, the great cluster of images we call Wisdom, and I lean for guidance on the apocryphal book of Ecclesiasticus because it offers a commentary on Job, chapter 28, as well as on a companion poem in Proverbs, chapter 8. We have to begin with a picture of wisdom as a wayside voice offering treasure beyond mere intelligence, power or wealth. That is fundamental. But *who* is wisdom, *what* is she? Ecclesiasticus says she is the voice of God's word, present with him before creation itself. She is there in the four rivers of life in our first Eden. She is heard in the Law given on Sinai. She journeys with the tabernacle or tent of God's pilgrim people and she completes her labour in a mighty Sabbath rest on Zion's holy mountain.

So our code book has offered us a family of resemblances: creation, Eden, law, pilgrim people, moving tabernacle, and Sabbath rest in the Jerusalem temple. You can, if you like, see this as sacred history and sacred geography like the landscapes and journeys Dante imagined as the way to the vision of God.

But we all know that when you have a close family of signs, altering one alters all, like a key change in music establishing a new centre. That is what happens as Christianity proclaims a divine foolishness wiser than the wisdom of men. As the wise men are diverted from Jerusalem to Bethlehem, wondering if this is 'all folly', they find divinity tabernacled in a child. What has been hidden from the wise has been revealed to babes. The holy spirit of divine folly cries out in the street, in the synagogue at Capernaum and in the Jerusalem temple, and is not heard. When Pilate puts the philosopher's question 'What is truth' it is the foolishness of God to say nothing because the answer comes soon enough in Pilate's own words: 'Behold the Man.' Divine wisdom is not an argument but love embodied.

Where, then, is wisdom to be found? In all her children who make up a living temple and inhabit a spiritual Zion where the original rivers of life once more flow freely, and the Lamb whose limbs were tied and trussed, is its temple and its light.

William Cowper brought all these themes together in a hymn based on the eighth chapter of Proverbs.

Ere God had built the mountains
  Or raised the fruitful hills;
Before He filled the fountains
  That feed the running rills;
In me, from everlasting
  The wonderful I AM
Found pleasures never wasting
  And Wisdom is my name.

When, like a tent to dwell in,
  He spread the skies abroad
And swathed about the swelling
  Of ocean's mighty flood.
He wrought by weight and measure,
  And I was with Him then;
Myself the Father's pleasure,
  And mine the sons of men.

Thus Wisdom's words discover
  Thy glory and thy grace
Thou everlasting lover
  Of our unworthy race;
Thy gracious eye surveyed us
  Ere stars were seen above;
In wisdom hast thou made us,
  And died for us in love.

Conversing with God

> Almighty and everlasting God who art always more ready to hear than we to pray, and art wont to give more than we deserve or desire; pour down upon us the abundance of thy mercy, forgiving us those things whereof our conscience is afraid, and giving us those good things we are not worthy to ask, but through the merits and mediation of Jesus Christ, thy Son our Lord.
>
> Collect for the twelfth Sunday after Trinity. *Book of Common Prayer.*

This collect, from the sacramentary of Pope Leo, is a prayer about prayer. It shows us how prayer is about our whole relationship with God. To have faith at all is to enter into an all-embracing condition of prayerfulness. And it is to begin with a certain kind of conversation.

I want to explore some parts of that conversation: how we question God and even put Him in question; how we learn to attend and recollect; how we respond to divine lucidity and tongues of fire; how we enter into the alignments of prayer and find the deepest solidarity in this precarious world.

How, then, do we question God? We have our precedents in the Psalms, which are part lyrics, part celebrations, part complaint and questioning.

Some of the most intense questioning of God comes in Psalm 22: 'My God, my God, why hast thou forsaken me? Why art thou so far from helping me, and from the words of my roaring?' More than half its thirty-one verses question God on account of his impotent absence. This is the most intimate conversation possible: why, if you exist, are you not here when I most need you? For some reason we are disturbed that our Saviour should repeat these words in the midst of his own agony, desolation and misery. But what just man or just woman can fail at some point to say 'My God, my God, why?' All through the Bible God is represented by his spokesmen as thundering safely from heaven about our inherited imperfections. But *this* prayer, this questioning cry of Psalm 22, turns the question round: where are *you*? George Herbert, poet and priest, called it 'reversed thunder', thunder sent back. Prayer, said Herbert, is the tower we place against the battlements of heaven to put our case on even terms and to hurl our complaint across. 'Engine 'gainst the Almighty, sinners' tower'.

Gerard Manley Hopkins, poet and priest, explored this part of the conversation to its most intimate and terror-stricken depths. He was, he says, 'past pitch of grief', falling over cliffs and through unfathomed space into an unbroken dark. His words lie directly parallel to those of Brian Keenan as he came out of years of physical and spiritual darkness as a hostage in Lebanon. Keenan spoke of the 'force of the fire' that is in man, of how man is 'a rare, unique beautiful creation'. He said also 'Hostage is a crucifying aloneness. It is a silent, screaming slide into the bowels of ultimate despair. Hostage is a man hanging by his fingernails over the edge of chaos, feeling his fingers slowly straightening.' Listen to Hopkins concluding his most terrified poem:

In the dark I lay wrestling with (my God) my God.

But it is not necessary for prayer to have any content whatever. It is possible simply to attend. The best conversations are often wordless: tangible not verbal. Prayer can be a silence in which God is Being itself, simply present. Or it can be a silence in which *we* are present, leaving aside all idea or thought of God. When we allow ourselves simply to be it is important to expect nothing in particular. Do not expect, do not shape, do not frame, do not name. Be dumb. Let go.

I was once in hospital with acute hypertension, wound up beyond any unwinding. On Sunday morning the last thing I wanted was a service, but I think the quietness of the time allowed self and world to move into mutual equilibrium. I noticed how my conscious self, chained to minutes, tasks and expectations, began to recede. 'I' became nothing but receptivity, an upturned bowl. Intention had become attention. I – but not I – attended to light slowly altering its angle through the window, to a wavering branch and its leaves, to low-level natural murmurs and cries, to greenness. I was absorbed in a lucidity I could not and must not name. George Herbert saw this condition as 'the land of spices. Something understood'.

This is the lucidity which comes when we consent to be dumb. It is not the only kind. Some while ago I was in Winchester Cathedral, shuffling around in the grey half-light. I was garnering information: the cathedral as record of campaigns and sufferings, people who died at sea or in the Crimea or Sudan or Afghanistan. I did not know a choir had secreted itself in the stalls, until suddenly the venerable spaces were traversed by perfect arcs of sound. This was prayer as incantation, the seraphim calling one to the other in the courts of the blessed.

O Lord open thou our lips
And our mouth shall show forth thy praise.

Lips can be dumb; lips can show forth praise. You never know when tongues of fire will fill all the house. One moment a building is a collection of memorials. The next it is transformed by lips that have been opened and mouths that show forth praise. 'My house shall be called a house of prayer.'

Prayer as contention; prayer as attention; prayer as incantation. But what finally of prayer as alignment and solidarity? Remember that the word 'precarious' literally means standing in the need of prayer. In 1985 my wife and I entered upon a few days of precariousness with people whose whole lives were precarious. A Lebanese Catholic priest came to the Worplesdon Hotel and asked me to join in a conversation with Muslims in Beirut. The visit is etched in my mind as sharply as acid; talks below ground-level in a sandbagged monastery, passionate and unending altercations in French and Arabic, cassettes of old Syrian melodies being played as we drove into the mountains overlooking the Bekaa Valley, the sight of churches brimming to the windows every night – and having to find in myself realistic words of hope. I recollect exhibiting the virtue of prudence. I declined an invitation to lecture at the American University in Muslim Beirut on 'The British stereotype of the Arab'.

But as the time to leave came we were increasingly conscious we had to go back across the 'green line' into the Beirut of Khomeini and Hizbollah. It was the only way out as it was the only way in. A Lebanese woman spoke to us with great care and earnestness just before we went and said, finally, 'In the union – *de la prière*'. This was her last line of communication, at that moment, or indeed at any time in all the long years of terror, and she was offering it to us for our brief moment of precariousness. It was an offer *to* us and a request for something *from* us; the union of prayer. This was not prayer as insurance, but prayer as calling to mind, as care and as solidarity.

Prayer, says Herbert, is 'the heart in pilgrimage': wrestling with God; letting go in order to see and hear; the opening of mouths to show forth praise; and it is holding each other, holding each other up, as we and our whole world stand always 'in the need of prayer'.

Divine Providence

O God, whose never-failing Providence ordereth all things in heaven and earth.
Collect for the Eighth Sunday after Trinity, *Book of Common Prayer.*

When I last preached at the Sung Eucharist, I took a hint from the original version of the Collect to reflect on the 'good things of time' – the *bona temporalia.* Today's Collect prompts me to preach a companion sermon on the much more difficult and dangerous topic of Providence – God's good acts in time. Unfortunately, the original version of today's Collect does little to ease the difficulty or reduce the danger. It runs 'O God, whose Providence never fails in the pursuit of its own'. I take that slightly mysterious phrase to mean that whatever the encroachments of chaos or nothingness the activity of Providence will not succumb to defeat. Or as Dame Julian of Norwich put it, 'All shall be well, and all manner of thing shall be well'.

That is quite difficult to believe, and yet to believe less may be a form of secret or unacknowledged atheism. I mean that it is not so difficult to respond to what we might call manifestations of divinity or traces of heaven, the winter lightning or the heart of a rose, because that requires nothing by way of divine activity. We can acknowledge God as perfect Being, as the Presence, but what He *does* is more problematic.

I once asked a colleague whether he supposed God *did* anything and he paused for rather a long time. What do you believe about God's sovereign activity? Is the world of nature and of history, including your own personal history day by day, an arena of God's Providence and never failing foresight, or is it a secular mosaic of closed connections and interactions? Of course, you and I still use phrases that echo belief in Providence at a distance, 'Thank God for that', we say or, 'That's a blessing.' If our plane limps home on one engine we might even say 'Thank God' with some fervour. But those are responses to what used to be called Special Providences, interventions in the likely order of events. And if we easily thank God for what we think He does, we may just as easily blame Him for what he allows, or does not. Providence more widely and truly understood is about God's consistent and persistent sustaining provision, power and purpose for us and the world. And maybe even in respect to that we are secret Wordsworthians, open to the mystery, responding to manifestations of spirit, even moved by the gift-giving of the Eucharist, but doubtful of a God revealed in his mighty acts or in the order of a never-failing Providence.

I know some people who do have just this sense of a divine hand, a tangible pressure active through the changes and chances of their lives. As they look back over their own biography they see a thread and acknowledge a power moulding or fashioning beyond their own direct initiative, yet not such as to obliterate their freedom or negate their personal responsibility. Others put it a little differently. They speak of placing their will within the will of God, and in doing that uncovering the purposes of Providence. I can feel with that, imaginatively. For such people dedication is a way of allowing Providence to show itself.

There are many variations on such experience. Goethe wrote that 'Providence has a thousand means to raise the fallen and support the prostrate. Sometimes our fate resembles a fruit tree in winter. Who would think at beholding so sad a sight that these rigid branches, these jagged twigs, would turn green again in the spring and blossom and bear fruit? But we hope it, we know it!' There are many people for whom the simple faith of the negro spiritual is quite enough: 'He's got the whole world in his hands.' We are moved by that because it comes from people whose terrible experience might teach them something very different.

I confess to a difficulty. I can feel with those meditative people who over years can trace providential threads, who have some sense of long-term fruition, prepared far back. But if this pattern can be true for them should it not be true for everybody? There my imagination fails. I look at the teeming myriad lives of this planet, some so short, some barely begun, some full to the bitter brim with frustration, some curtailed to the barest minimum by disease, some spiralling out of control to spiritual destruction. Could they have such a comforting sense of never-failing Providence? What providential fruition for the fifteen-year-old shrivelled to death by bombing?

Yet the Gospel is clear, and the world of that time was no kinder, no less flat contrary to any faith in a never-failing Providence. Your heavenly Father careth for you. There is a special Providence in the fall of a sparrow. Are you not worth more than many sparrows? All the hairs of your head are numbered. What greater assurance of an all-embracing care?

Perhaps we have only two serious options. We can reduce God to the Creator who merely set off the Big Bang and then retired from all active involvement. This God went into very early retirement after a brilliant start. The face of such a God, says R.S. Thomas, is quite inhuman. It is just 'the face of a clock', and his work is no more than the invisible instructions carried by our genes or the practices of an 'abstruse geometry that proceeds eternally in the silence beyond right and wrong'. That pares God back to energies and laws and principles. The Christian alternative is to envisage One who is in all and through all, pursuing a rich consummation, prohibiting total defeat or absolute nullity or irredeemable frustration. This Creator would request and need the engagement and cooperation of the creature. And addressed in this way we would not be playthings of the combination of the elements nor would we be playthings of an all-encompassing divine predestination. We would become cooperators in a divine project.

Supposing we cast our vote for a Providence that will not in the end be frustrated or permit the triumph of the lie. And supposing we see ourselves as cooperating with that Providence. Then the spirit in which we live, its tenor, its grain, its temper, will follow suit. We will strive for largeness of mind and heart, and *so far as we can* exercise a precise care and foresight, but we will not be eaten away by anxiety. We will always recollect the limits of our responsibility. We will look for the creative and redeeming possibility in every occasion, but we will know also that we *have* a Creator and Redeemer. We do not need to know what the consummation will be, because it is enough to be in continuity and connected.

Fénelon, a wise spiritual director in seventeenth-century France, gave this advice to himself:

[Cheered] by the presence of God, I will do at each moment, without anxiety, according to the strength which he shall give me, the work that his Providence assigns. I will leave the rest without concern; it is not my affair … I ought to consider the duty to which I am called each day, as the work God has given me to do, and to apply myself to it in a manner worthy of his glory, that is to say *with exactness and in peace.*

Infection and Re-creation

> Because the creation itself *also* shall be delivered from the bondage of corruption into the glorious liberty of the sons of God.
>
> St Paul's Epistle to the Romans, chapter 8, verse 21.

In this text St Paul has a vision of a restored creation, a natural world unbound, uncorrupted, uninfected by sin. Lying behind this vision is an idea of some aboriginal disaster in which humankind and nature shared a common mysterious fall. As the consequences of the fall in man are reversed, so the consequences of the fall in nature are to be reversed. Death and decay gained dominion over humankind and nature; in the fullness of time death and decay shall have no more dominion.

I confess I find the idea difficult as it stands. I do not know what to make of the direct link between sin understood as a corruption of our human nature, and decay understood as a corruption of the natural world. And it follows that I am equally uneasy about the direct link between the conquest of sin and the abolition of physical corruption. I accept Paul's great contrast between the first and the second Adam, the one falling into corruption and the other redeeming humankind from corruption, because I can see both as belonging to our human and moral world: a profound infection of our condition is matched by a profound restorative. But that *nature* directly picked up that infection as part of the aboriginal disaster and that nature will be directly restored as part of a full working out of redemption I find difficult. Unhappily that means I cannot simply expound the text, and I have also to undertake a dangerous solo flight of my own.

The problem with Paul's direct link between human sin and the onset of decay or degeneration is that it not only makes death a matter of human fault but leads on to the idea that we suffer now by a kind of extended and inevitable genetic contagion. It seems important to me to regard decay as a natural process quite disconnected from human agency. Diseases are not malign visitations inherently and universally derived from some moral malignity, either of the race or of the individual, in the past or now. The natural world and its processes are morally neutral. In any case, to abolish decay is to stultify new life and novelty. It arrests the whole cycle of nature. Do we really want trees that never shed leaves or people who never beget? Can we even imagine a world where nothing is changeful or precarious?

So I have a major problem: how to discard part of Paul's frame and yet maintain the central assertion concerning this dual restoration of the human substance and of the natural world. For Paul asserts beyond all doubt the existence of a *movement* from fear to love, from bondage to sonship, from alienation to intimate trust, which is also a movement in the re-creation of the cosmos closer to the image of the Maker. That restoration is to come about through the co-operation of the human spirit of re-creation and the divine Spirit of re-creation.

How then can I reframe so sublime an affirmation? To do so I must step back and recollect that the world is a universe and not a multi-verse, and that it everywhere issues in order. There is a moral order and a natural order. To flout or ignore order in either the one or the other makes fruitfulness impossible. Natural fruitfulness and human fruition depend on some kind of reasoning reflective response to *rule*. To cheat, deceive, destroy, dishonour, is to invite moral destruction. To ignore the rules of nature is to invite physical destruction and to make a desert where the rose should bloom and the vineyard flourish. So the two spheres have some connection, though not through the direct and aboriginal contagion understood by Paul. The moral corruption of human beings, not only their greed and rapacity but their disrespect for order, spills over in the exhaustion and depletion of nature. Of course, it is all much more complicated than that. Greed, corruption and violence have mixed with creativity to concentrate marvellous deposits of richness: a Venice or a Constantinople. Even so there is a profound level at which the rules of the moral world and the rules of the natural world intersect.

Perhaps I can come at this in a slightly different way. There is in the human and in the natural world a discernible beggary, a crack, a strange lack, a sense of something blasted. This sense of something blasted is both something already *there*, deep-set and long-lasting, *and* something *we* exacerbate by an additional or surplus perversity. In the moral world we easily identify what it is to be blasted. We recognize a deep-seated fracture, an incapacity and a bondage, and a perverse self-seeking which is indifferent to hurt. In the natural world I am less sure how we might express the sense of something blasted. Henry Vaughan in his great poem 'Corruption' wrote of nature as 'quarrelsome' and estranged. And yet Vaughan also spoke of nature as infiltrated by gleams and celestial hints. I can only express it myself in terms of a bareness, a deficit and sometimes a raw deformation. My difficulty is in picking up this bareness, and this 'absence'; and yet I know that the recalcitrance of nature is not to be identified with deformation and that human ingenuity can work most marvellously upon that recalcitrance. One thing is certain, however, and that is the way the disaster in the moral world, what Paul calls 'bondage', can spill over into natural disaster. So much is unrealized, laid waste or consigned to waste, beggared by indifference, polluted, hurt, depleted by rapacity. The shrinking and lifeless Aral Sea is a parable of misuse and disrespect.

So how then are we to uncover and achieve fullness and consonance? How do we make things human and natural 'sound together' and fulfil themselves? For that let me use a poem of W.H. Auden who was able truly to imagine what a linkage of our moral world and the natural order might be, and to devise an equivalent of Paul's vision. Auden turned first, as I have done, to the universality of order. There is, he says, a 'single glory' springing from the divine Word, which underlies all order, moral or natural. Redemption in the moral world is a 'cleansing', what he calls 'cleansed occasions'. Redemption in the natural world is rendering a fabric 'intact'. And the two become united, as he puts it, in terms of 'cleansed occasions in accord together, as one feeling fabric all flushed and intact'. The visionary quest is to seek the cleansed and the intact. The cleansed and the intact, he says, sound together in one 'Multitudinous oecumenical song' of gratitude and joy.

The Imageless and the Human Face of God

And the glory of the Lord shall be revealed, and all flesh shall see it together.
Isaiah, chapter 10, verse 5.

Some years ago I was absorbed in a strange personal transition: from being in Egypt to being in England, also from the temples of Egyptian God-Kings and from the mosques of Cairo to this luminous season of Advent and Christmas. It is difficult to convey the immense distance I have travelled, which is far greater than a mere five hours' plane journey. It is a journey through several thousand years from the worship of natural and imperial power expressed in the imposing and the colossal to the season of the Holy Child. And it is a journey from a stark imageless monotheism without a human face to a faith actually centred on the redemptive activity of a human being. Islam is the expression of the Perfect Word, the holy located in the Book; Christianity is the Word made flesh. It is not so much a contrast between Mohammed and Christ, though the Saviour is profoundly different from the Prophet, as between two kinds of divine Word, one written, one enacted in a birth, a life and a death.

There is another contrast, which separates Christian believing equally from Islam and from ancient Egyptian religion, and that is in the understanding and the place of Power. Christianity turns on an oxymoron, that figure of speech which places two opposed ideas together: when I am weak I am strong, when I fall I rise. The Christian holds that divine strength was and is perfected in human weakness. In Islam and in Ancient Egypt God suffers no human weakness. For Islam God may be compassionate and merciful as well as powerful but this mercy is not expressed in a human passion, such as the Passion of Christ. Christians gather around the meal of their dying Saviour; Muslims kneel rank upon rank before the immutable infinitude of the Eternal One and his Perfect Word. Here is no body of a child and here is no broken body of a Man. In Islam the Christian sign of finitude and brokenness and suffering divinity is the great Absence. For Christianity it is the great Presence.

Of course, there is much in Christianity which speaks of Power: power in nature and in the order of the physical world, power in the order of the social world. God is a ruler and a mighty King and our human rulers and kings can be viceroys of his power. In the great icons of Eastern Christianity, in San Vitale, Ravenna, you find earthly kingship placed in partnership with heavenly kingship.

So, of course, there *is* natural and communal power channelled through Christianity, just as there is a sense of immemorial fatality and the reproduction and rotation of the ceaseless round. All those elements in our natural and social environment which speak of ordination and unchangeable rotation find a voice within Christianity. God the Father Almighty is the Maker of heaven and earth.

That is the very first article of the Christian creed. Indeed, for some people it is the last article as well as the first. Yet everything that is distinctive and redemptive about Christianity is conveyed in a human life, death and resurrection. The unique good news has to do with the human love of God.

The question of belief in the incarnation is not the first question we should ask ourselves. That is not the way into this mystery. To enter into Christianity we need rather to open ourselves up to what is presented in the picture of the child and the wounded man. We have to allow an idea of God to be reformed in the shape of a baby: the joyful uniqueness of the holy child and the final isolation of the redemptive Man. We need to experience this as God's *kindness*: His being one of our *kind*, His being housed in humanity, taking up His *abode* and making His *dwelling* with His people. 'The Lord hath visited and redeemed His people.'

As we approach the great feasts of Christianity, the celebration of divinity under a human roof, the solemn recollection of divinity undergoing and overcoming a human death, we need to absorb *pictures* and identify with a *narrative*. God as He is presented to us by faith is in picture and story rather than principle and proposition. Without picture and story our idea of God recedes into an impersonal vacuum of the Great Artificer, Supreme Architect and Perfect Mathematician. His face is obliterated, whitewashed out in geometry and abstraction and repetition. But with picture and story He is humanity and vulnerability and uniqueness. His power is realized through the most amazing of all pictures, which is the human figure and face. The manifestation of the spirit is in the body, the word made flesh.

Above all, it is a broken body, heavy and suspended, which becomes for us the pre-eminent and all-embracing sign of God's grace and mercy. In a mosque there is no bread signifying the body of Christ offered to humankind, no cross signifying the involvement of divinity in suffering unto death. Nobody salutes a true body or absorbs a human gift. There is just prayer and word, prostration and proclamation.

What we have then in this Christianity is the offer of the infant king, whose strength is made perfect in weakness. If we were to absorb just the power of the imageless potentate we would either assimilate ourselves to that power or else prostrate ourselves before it. But by fixing our eyes on cradle and cross we alter the meaning of power, allowing it to work through our nature and through the gift of the body. Christmas is about the gift of the self conveyed in the body of Christ.

Good Things

[May we] so pass through things temporal that we finally lose not the things eternal.
Collect for the Fourth Sunday after Trinity, *Book of Common Prayer.*

The collects in our Prayer Book are a kind of abbreviated divinity, the heart of Christian reflection displayed in miniature. Collects bring together or 'collect' a thought for the day. They are also word music of a holy spirit, because devotion always finds a pulse in which to express itself. Collects breathe, and to speak them carefully is to enter into a kind of pure and peaceable wisdom. That is what the word 'inspiration' literally means: being breathed into by the divine wisdom.

Just occasionally some element in that wisdom has been lost in translation. Our Collects come, of course, from collections of Latin prayers which were composed anonymously in the early centuries of the Church. Sometimes the reformers improved or purified these prayers, sometimes they missed real touches of devotional imagination. Consider, for example, the privilege and profit of being able to pray 'O God, who art the author of peace and lover of concord, in knowledge of whom standeth our eternal life, whom to serve is to reign: *cui servire regnare est*. Consider the thoughts which might be provoked by the original version of the Collect for today, 'May we so pass through *the good things of time* that we finally lose not the good things of eternity'. I want to think about those good things of time.

What did this anonymous Christian mean by what he called the '*bona temporalia*': the good things of time? And what did all those faithful people who used this prayer throughout the medieval centuries mean by the 'good things of time'? It is not as if their lives were crammed with good things. Their bodies, their homes and their towns were ridden with dirt and disease, they met constant poverty and misfortune; and their lives were short. Our ancestors endured lordly exaction and judicial savagery, and revenged themselves on each other without a qualm. Animals existed mainly for food or as beasts of burden, not for cherishing. Nature was for the most part merely captious or threatening, and you wrested such living from it as you could. How often then did they consider the lilies of the field or lift their eyes up to the hills or watch the rising or setting sun? These good things so precious to us perhaps stayed at the corner of their vision.

And yet most of the things they considered good are what we too consider good: the mutual love of man and woman, of parents and offspring; the sight of children's children; peace; good neighbours, good company, and good friends; good health, good weather, safe journeyings, and plentiful harvests; Spring; abundance of herds and flocks, and fish and fowl; the pleasures of the table, and occasions of feasting and celebration; the possession of hearth and home; skill, and craftsmanship; the sounds of music and delight of dancing. I am not thinking here of the virtues or the courtesies or the most excellent gift of charity, but of bounty, sheer bounty.

Each of us could lovingly enumerate our own 'good things of time'. When I asked a Scottish colleague he suggested 'fresh salmon on a May morning'. But what about the book: opening it, handling it, burying yourself in it as a work of art and a repository of intelligence? What about window boxes and flowers in the hearth? What about the aroma of a 'good thing' that strikes you on entering the workshop of an instrument maker, or of some lover of intricate and serviceable shapes, and of ingenious solutions? Polished woods and grateful textures are good; so is the sound of running water and sunlight on the hill's shoulder; so is the absorbed expression of a child. These make up the infinite variety of delights, provided you don't have toothache or are driven mad with anxiety and care.

The proper love of the 'good things of time' is something that poets understand and celebrate. They are the loving enumerators, high priests in the celebration of bounty. Rupert Brooke, for example, enumerated some of the 'good things of time' in his poem 'The Great Lover':

> These I have loved:
> White plates and cups, clean-gleaming,
> Ringed with blue lines; and feathery, faery dust;
> Wet roofs, beneath the lamp-light; the strong crusts
> Of friendly bread; and many-tasting food;

If you go through the writings of Gerard Manley Hopkins they are mostly startled ejaculations at the exuberant beauty of the world. He lets out something between a cry and a shout about the mastery of a bird in flight; a pastoral forehead in Wales; sweet earth, sweet landscapes and low grass; clouds jostling in their airy thoroughfares; loose locks and the grace of girls, eye lashes, airs by Henry Purcell. And most wonderful of all, for him and for us, the human face as register of selfhood: the face in innocence, the face in venerability, in care, in love, in absorption. The visage of man is the most mobile and complete index of what any divinity must be: the face of the maker, the lover, and the giver. No wonder we humans have been given our most persuasive knowledge of God 'in kind', in our own kind, in the face of one of ourselves. It is here that the good things of time are caught clearly in the aspect of eternity.

And yet, in spite of these 'goods' our hearts fail us for fear and uncertainty: fear of transiency, our own and those we love, and uncertainty because the signals given out by the world are so ambiguous. Nature is deeply fissured, treacherous as well as inviting, and blighted as well as fecund; humanity is cracked and split, as much twisted as straight and whole; the human city is as much Babylon as it is Jerusalem.

No wonder we are of two minds: unable to live with the hope of God and unable to be resolutely hopeless. Certainly I am not myself among the sure and steadfast partisans of promise. It is as if we recollect some Paradise on the other side of the forbidding fence and can overhear some scrambled but promising message, and yet inwardly we are broken by the weight of unintelligibility and dissolution. The sons and daughters of God cry out with joy at first light on the first day and we cry with them, and yet we have acquired some other deadly and unassuageable sorrow. Indeed, some of the most miraculous of the good things of time are infiltrated with just this creaturely sorrow. They allow the springs of joy to mingle so freely with the springs of sadness as though the presage of loss were part of the real presence of perfection. Perhaps it is. Perhaps that is how things are in the deeply reconciled realm. Perhaps the good things of time are what they seem, good in themselves and also affirmative, fulfilled and promising, but above all bathing the wound of sorrow in the fount of joy.

Bedevilment and Delivery

> But if I with the finger of God cast out devils no doubt the Kingdom of God is come upon you.
>
> St Luke's Gospel, chapter 11, verse 20

How do we, in the contemporary world, read a story about the exorcism of a dumb devil? Of course, there are some people who do not bat an eyelid, and simply go and do likewise. I have a good friend, William Abraham, D.Phil. (Oxon) who does just that. One of his female students in Dallas, where he teaches, harboured an unruly sub-self who (or which) started to spit out obscenities in his lectures on the philosophy of religion. Billy judged that on rational grounds these comments were unjustified. A semi-jocular conversation followed between Billy and the demon, who eventually confessed to some curious name, whereupon Billy ordered it (or him or her) to depart in the name of Christ and never to trouble his student more.

The early Church, or indeed the Church at any time up to the eighteenth century, would not have been surprised by Billy. The rite of baptism in the early Church was preceded by exorcism, in order first to banish the evil spirits before the believer passed through the cleansing waters. St Jerome, gaunt and alone in his cave, translating the Bible into Latin, fended off all assaults of the world, the flesh *and* the devil, and put down Satan under his feet. He knew, as the early Church knew, that the 'principalities' and powers that had split off from God's kingdom – and who (or which) exercised dominion in our fallen world – were in the end subject to Christ. For that matter the cantatas of J.S. Bach are replete with images of spiritual warfare.

From time to time, my wife and I left the Guildford of the late twentieth century to carry out research in Latin America among tens of millions of Pentecostal Christians who live in the New Testament. I have no doubt those people are dramatically renewed in body as well as soul and are empowered to meet the appalling circumstances of life in the shanty towns of Rio or Santiago or Guatemala City. They talk to us quite naturally about healings and exorcisms, and about turning to the omnipotent Friend of Souls to expel the potent Enemy of Souls and rid them of demonic possession.

Not everyone agrees with them, or with Billy Abraham or with the Church before the scientific enlightenment. Plenty of people believe that we today have a correct understanding of these things and the right psychological or medical terminology, such as dual personality, compulsion, ill-defined boundaries to the self, regression, trauma, projection. Professor Dennis Nineham, a while ago, suggested that the New Testament itself belonged irretrievably to the archaic past. For him there are some things a modern man cannot believe. A great gulf is fixed between our North Atlantic pond of rationality and the rest of time and humanity.

In some ways Dennis Nineham must be right. There is a crucial difference brought about by modern science. But when it comes to the realm of the spirit, to the demonic, or to healings and restorations for that matter, I don't myself believe the New Testament lies on the other side of a great gulf. Rather I believe we and the New Testament share a common experience, a common sense, a common language, with human beings at all times and in all places.

The *realities* of that older world, and the *power* of its language, are still with us. And that is not merely because newspapers briefly tell us that *elsewhere*, in Cardiff or Liverpool, there are demonic deteriorations of a most appalling kind. The universal past is present *here*, and it haunts our language. 'I can't imagine what possessed me'; 'He (or she) was a monster in human form'; 'The soldiers went berserk and acted like mad dogs'; 'Are you out of your mind?'; 'I completely lost my self-possession.' Today's headline reads: 'Racist demons running loose all over Europe.' In our dreams old unquiet layers of our minds crumple and open up to allow nameless spirits of fear or destruction to roam the recesses. The sanitized surface buckles under primeval pressure.

Some time ago, I read an article by a psychiatrist about child abuse in which he openly admits that clinical language fails him. He begins to revert to an older stronger form of speech. 'I read ... about ... helpless children under the tyranny of monstrous parents ... of the killing of love and the murder of souls ... of people whose inner self has been so blasted away that they are in a state of steady stupor.' Dr Shengold suggests that the technical terms we rightly devise to achieve distance and to put indignation aside in order to better understand have at some point to give place to another language, and once we as *humans* stand face to face with murder, murder in and murder of the soul, we have to recover that language without forfeiting our modernity. Of course, I have never seen the seven goodly spirits of wisdom and love, except on the index of the human face. Nor have I seen the seven deadly demons of death and destruction except on the index of the human face. But there is a volcanic fault line in our moral universe and a splitting off of disorderly powers over and over again resurgent in our individual lives. Some of these powers, deep down, lie so close to the divine energy we rightly acknowledge that 'I the Lord create light and dark, make good and evil'. That is why prophets and creative minds so often walk a diminishing ledge of reason. Other unearthly powers are engaged in unremitting pursuit of destruction, dominion and eternal death. In between are parodies of God, some enticing and close as, for example, sexuality as love-death in Wagner's *Tristan*, some far from their original, yet still strangely reminiscent as when sex is played out as total omnipotence or ecstatic humiliation.

That is why Satan has so many names: Lucifer, the light bearer, who lost his footing and has to feed our stolen reality; or Beelzebub, (literally) the lord of the flies and the dung, Enemy of good and Father of lies. As for the demons, their name is legion, but they roam a landscape of spiritual deterioration; the waste, the ruin, the cemetery. They are dark, driven energies, eyes averted or vacant, sovereign reason dethroned or endangered, atomizing beings eating into integrity, real absences, head over heels in hatred or self-love. They are every way in which human beings may be blasted, stolen away, preyed upon, eaten up and cannibalized. And all of this has to be possible in a universe where free spirits choose God for Himself alone, and where He pays the cost of redemption through His humanity and not merely through His sovereign power.

Age-old dis-ease, age-old remedy. Planted in human experience are emblems or signs of a different kingdom, ordering chaos, recovering waste, reversing destruction, delivering from prison, offering healing and restoring and renewing creation. We can align ourselves with these signs wherever we meet them, above all the sign of the cross and the holy name. That means we share love's meal where reality is not stolen but given, where no-one is eaten up by greed but all sustained by grace.

For to be in communion with each other at common tables is to witness, so far as is possible for such frail ambiguous creatures, that neither death nor life, nor angels, nor principalities, nor powers, nor things present, nor things to come, nor height nor depth, nor any other creature, shall be able to separate us from the love of God.

Descending and Ascending: A Homily

> Friend, go up higher ... for whoever exalts himself shall be humbled, and he that humbles himself shall be exalted.
>
> St Luke's Gospel, chapter 14, verses 10–11.

On the face of it the point of the story about not risking humiliation by going straight to the top table when invited to a banquet looks like canny advice. But if we take into consideration all three phases in Luke's account of the Lord's Sabbath-day meal with a prominent Pharisee, we find we have the key notes of the gospel.

The first phase about Jesus healing the man with dropsy affirms that the Sabbath and its rules were made for man; the second phase about not seeking out the top table focusses in the end on the profound saying about the casting down of the proud and the exaltation of the humble; the third phase is a kind of extension of that because it emphasizes yet again the great reversals of the kingdom since those who ought really to be invited to a feast are not the well-heeled but the poor, the blind and the maimed.

If we fasten on the text about the strange reversals awaiting the humble and the exalted it is plainly the lynch-pin of everything else. In love's kingdom, both within us and mysteriously 'at hand', it is the Lord who washes the feet of the servant and it is the servant girl who is filled with grace to become exalted among women. The one who comes among us incognito in the form of a servant is also the risen Lord. He that descended is also he that ascended. So from a story about a banquet to the incarnation itself the pattern of descent and ascent is the same.

But which among us is able to bear this truth and follow the narrow path to 'life abundant'? Are we at all likely to make a gift of self? For the most part we are 'broad way' people, seeking selfish ends, pursuing self-expression. We take what looks the easy and natural way, except that maybe in the long run that exacts its own costs. Peer Gynt in Ibsen's play spends his whole life looking for a true self only to find nothing at the centre, pure self-defeat, the hole in the heart. It is then that he overhears the gospel warning, 'he that would save his life shall lose it'.

Where then does that leave us intermittently decent 'broad way' people? The answer is: included by grace. Love's strange doctrine is as tender as it is demanding. On the one hand everything is expected; on the other all is forgiven. Merely to seek is to find; merely to knock is to find the door of heaven mysteriously opened. Though by the law you are very far from the kingdom, by grace it is there for the asking. Indeed, we may not even need to knock, because it is the servant-Lord himself who stands at the door and knocks and asks if *He* may sup with *us*.

> We give Thee thanks
>   for Thy mercy
> that we are not consumed ...
> that it is from everlasting to everlasting
> reacheth to Heaven, reacheth to hell ...

pardoning unto seventy times seven …
standing at the door and knocking
the Lord Himself entreating His own servants,
Thou, whose place is the Throne of Grace,
    the Mercy-seat,
    whose time is the Day of Salvation.

(Lancelot Andrewes)

Signs of New Creation

Whereas I was blind now I see.

St. John's Gospel, chapter 9, verse 25.

When John Drury at Christchurch, Oxford visited Guildford Cathedral to talk about the nature of the signs in the gospels, such as the feeding of the five thousand, some people accused him of making the gospels complicated. The truth is that the gospels have plain meanings and deeper symbolic meanings. When it comes to being 'wise to salvation' the good news could not be more transparent, but when it comes to entering into their full meaning matters can be more challenging. Many Christians are puzzled by aspects of the gospels as when a friend asked me distinctly awkward questions about the water converted into wine at the wedding in Cana.

In this particular story of the blind man healed by the pool of Siloam we all understand the phrase 'Whereas I was blind now I see', but being blind and having your eyes opened are also spiritual conditions. There is sight and there is insight. This is a story of light and enlightenment. We need to hear the obvious meaning and overhear the wider meanings. Otherwise we, too, 'have eyes and see not'.

To overhear those meanings better we need to place this sign of God's glory in the ninth chapter of John alongside the wider sevenfold pattern of signs in the first half of his gospel, which runs from the first sign at the wedding in Cana to the last sign in the resurrection of Lazarus. In each 'showing forth' of glory we see the Eternal Word of the prologue of John's gospel manifest in time. Spirit is fleshed out before our eyes. In the wedding at Cana Christ is the new wine that comes last; in the meeting with the woman of Samaria by the well he is the living water; in the feeding of the multitude he is the bread of life; and in the raising of Lazarus he is the resurrection and the life. In the story of the man cured of blindness Christ is the light of the world. That light is 'the true light' suffusing the whole of John's gospel.

In the Prologue to St. John the Eternal Word, unnameable and unutterable, enters our world to receive a name. As in Harrison Birtwistle's opera 'The Last Supper' the 'I am' becomes flesh and dwells among us under names we recognise in our daily experience: 'I am ... the Good shepherd', 'I am ... the Living Bread'. And he has two special names which humanise divinity: Son of God and Son of Man. To address God and know him under these names *is* Christianity. That is why every Christian prayer is in and through the name. Towards the end of the story of the healing of the blind man, Jesus asks him if he believes in the Son of God. The answer comes back 'Who is he?' and Jesus answers 'You have *seen* him'. Whereas he was blind now he sees.

The depth of meaning in the sign displayed in chapter 9 comes out if we compare it with the sign displayed in chapter 5 where the crippled man is healed by the pool of Bethesda. St. John is showing how the kingdom comes each time men and women are unbound and made whole. We walk in the light of the new creation by the power of the living Word. As St. Mark also says the kingdom comes because the lame walk, the blind receive their sight, the ears of the deaf are unstopped, and the dumb sing.

At this point I want to speak more personally because if sign and image are central to the New Testament then it has to be read as a kind of narrative poetry. In the Scripture we encounter types and symbols and emblems of transfiguration, and that is how the early Church which created the New Testament understood its own creation. What stands in the way of that are, first, the so-called critical method, which disintegrates the text into a thousand pieces without seeing it steady and seeing it whole, but also its mirror image in fundamentalism, which understands the New Testament about as much as a flat-earther understands the expanding universe.

I have always been reluctant to describe the New Testament as a narrative poem because people too easily think poetry is a matter of lines and rhymes and confuse works of the imagination with what is imaginary. Yet we are continually speaking of the image of God made flesh in the face of Christ and in the living water, bread and wine. That is poetry or, if you prefer, communication by signs. Moreover, this central *image* of the human face of Christ, transfigured and marred, is not a closed work but a frame in which we place ourselves to cooperate in new creation. The word 'poet' means maker, and the poem of Scripture not only offers insight into the mind of the Maker but room to engage creatively with the script. The New Testament invites us to make the Word a real presence in the world of our daily bread.

Les Murray in his latest collection of poems entitled 'Learning Human' writes

> 'Religions are poems. They concert our
> daylight and dreaming mind, our emotions,
> instinct, breath and native gesture
> into the only whole thinking: poetry'.

'Whole thinking' gives us the clue because by involving every part of us it enables us to be made whole and so to 'learn human'. Les Murray also writes that 'Full religion' must be 'inexhaustable', always inviting us to ask 'Now why did the poet do that?' So faith is a fresh horizon, an anticipation, a novel possibility, a second birth, a different city, a vista beyond wilderness and chaos. Faith is not a set of recited formulae, even though we need them to stabilise our thoughts and to think with, but an act of uncovering whereby the eyes of the blind are opened, the ears of the deaf are unstopped and those long silent find a tongue of fire.

Of course, we modern Christians are often like Nicodemus who came hesitantly and querulously to the light by night. Yet the New Testament is a proclamation not a query, and celebrates the Spirit at work in restoring light in the heart of darkness. It unveils signs of the great transition from first creation to second, from fallen to restored, and from the binding power of darkness to the glorious liberty of those in the light and the truth.

> 'The Lord is my light and my salvation …
> of whom then shall I be afraid?'

Part III
Emergent Occasions: Celebration and Mourning in Sacred Spaces

Banner 7 – The Seventh Day: The Day of Rest
Taken from *The Creation: The Banners of Winchester Cathedral* by Thetis Blacker, Friends of Winchester Cathedral, 2001.

Emergent Occasions: Celebration and Mourning in Sacred Spaces

In spite of the inevitable reincorporation of Christianity in the hierarchies of power belonging to the old dispensation and the City of Man, what is still guarded in the holy place at the sacred heart of the secular city? There is, first of all, the perpetual recollection of exemplary witnesses, imitating the sacrifice of Christ. These are martyrs who put their bodies on the line and take on themselves the violence of Church and State. There is the enshrining of the heart's reasons against *raison d'état* – and peaceful demonstrations (or walks to the gates of the city) till the walls of division come tumbling down – Berlin, South Africa. There is the demarcation of templates of sacred space where people meet solely as people to celebrate what matters more than the wealth of banks or the power of governments. In these sacred spaces times are set apart for celebration and mourning: celebration through music which manifests the perfect within the ruined, or celebration of intimate human love in the context of divine charity; and mourning which faces the reality of the body and the altars stripped of everything except for one solitary light of hope.

Commemoration of Martyrs[1]

> Gold is tried in the fire.
>
> Ecclesiasticus, chapter 2, verse 5.

> We are compassed about with so great a cloud of witnesses ...
>
> Epistle to the Hebrews, chapter 12, verse 1.

Among those witnesses in the University of Cambridge we name:

Robert Barnes, John Lambert, John Frith, martyred under Henry
Bishops Latimer and Ridley, martyred under Mary
Archbishop Cranmer, martyred under Mary

To which we add other martyred representatives of conscience:

Ann Askew, Reformed, martyred under Henry
Thomas More, Catholic, martyred under Henry
Joan Boshcr, Unitarian, martyred under Edward
John Penry, separatist, martyred under Elizabeth
Robert Southwell, Catholic, martyred under Elizabeth

What is a martyr? He or she is a witness to a truth so overriding it demands the stand of last resort. Martyrdom arises out of a clash between conscience and power, the reasons of the heart and mind pitted against reasons of state and Church. For state and Church there is opportunity to control heart and mind by breaking the body; for the protester – the Protestant – the body has to be mastered for the sake of integrity. The body is broken that the heart may stay whole. In the eyes of the inquisitor the heart of the protester is the site of a malignant disease capable of infecting the whole body of society and destroying its integrity; for the protest-ant his heart is the Ark of a New Covenant sealed with his blood.

Usually there is a trial in every sense of that word. Martyrs are tried to prove them publicly wrong; they also undergo many trials to prove *themselves* in the fires of affliction. For the inquisitor the trial is before the majesty of the law; for the martyr it is before another court and a different judge. Martyrs are sustained because they take their stand in two different tribunals, one with a first judgement trying the mind and body, the other with the last judgement concerning the soul. The earthly court tries to prove a case against the martyr, whereas the martyr knows he or she is tried, proved and approved by God. Precious metal is proved in the fire.

When martyrs face their accusers they are confronting a panoply of assembled power. Luther, for example, when he faced the assembled powers of Europe at the Diet of Worms initially blenched and took a day to recover his voice to say, '*Hier ich stehe, ich kann nicht anders*'. The inner strength of the one who is alone tries conclusions with the outward strength of the many and is taunted, 'See how many they are that witness against you'. A strange parody of debate occurs, the object of which is not truth but entrapment, between the one who is disarmed and the armed multitude, where the accused has to answer for himself and the accusers do not. There is no chance to say, 'I also will ask you a question.' There is opportunity only to answer them nothing and then be struck on the mouth for silence. You must choose when to be dumb, when to say, 'You say so', and when the time has come to make the good confession. When Cranmer stood trial there were times when he replied, 'You say so', and other times when there were mysterious omissions. Once the moment came to speak he was allowed just half a dozen sentences before closure, but they contained everything he wanted to say and everything they needed to know. It was enough, and immediately they harried and hurried him to the place of execution. Similarly, Thomas More under constant inquisition, kept silence, saying neither Yea nor Nay to Henry's supremacy over the Church, before taking his stand on the 'common and known' tradition of Catholic Christendom. He told his sorrowing wife the Tower of London was as close to heaven as Chelsea. The trial is the weapon of whoever holds power. Nevertheless, even subjects have their say.

It is precisely because the accusers need to show you are wrong that you are given that brief moment to show you are right. This is one kind of demonstration against another kind of demonstration, the personal sentence pronounced against the legal sentence, the witness confronting the witnesses. For the authorities part of the demonstration is a disgrading in which you are divested of everything that is properly yours in order that you may be reduced to a man or a woman without properties.

They took the Primate of All England and stripped him of all that signified his office. By reducing him to a body they made of him a nobody and an outcast. They did with him whatsoever they would. He was cast out of the land of the living, outlawed into a no man's land.

Yet the martyr while he lives still has a body. Perhaps there is a chance for one gesture, as when Cranmer thrust the hand that signed his recantation first into the fire. Perhaps there is a chance for one last sentence as when Latimer called to his fellow bishop, 'Be of good cheer Master Ridley and play the man, for we shall this day light such a fire in England as shall never be put out'. Even when pinioned and naked the body itself is the martyr's remaining voice. The wounding and the scarring speak for themselves. This is my body and this is my blood. Behold the Man. Behind every martyr's trial is that trial of trials where, in the broken man, placarded before us, we meet the glance of the King of Kings and Lord of Lords.

Martyrs are fortified by an unseen peaceful army of those who fought the good fight and finished the course. In that last desolation little remains but to recollect the great cloud of witnesses. In memory and in anticipation the past and future are called in to outweigh the present: the confirmation of testimony by Abraham, Barak and all the prophets. Every 'heir of promise' is 'looking unto Jesus, who for the joy that was set before him endured the cross, despising the shame'.

After death the martyr goes on speaking. These are the words of Ann Askew from Newgate Prison in 1546. It is her own 'Imitation of Christ'.

Not oft use I to write
In prose nor yet in rhyme
Yet I will show one sight
That I saw in my time.

I saw a royal throne
Where Justice should have sit,
But in her stead was one
of moody cruel wit.

Absorbed was righteousness
As of the raging flood
Satan in his excess
Sucked up the guiltless blood.

Then thought I, Jesus Lord,
When thou shalt judge us all,
Hard is it to record
On these men what will fall.

Yet, Lord, I thee desire
For that they did to me,
Let them not taste the hire
Of their iniquity.

Note

1 St Edward's, Cambridge.

Commemoration of Tyndale's Birth: 1494–1536

> Behold I shewe you a mystery …
>
> St Paul's First Epistle to the Corinthians, chapter 15, verse 5.

These are the words of William Tyndale translating the words of St Paul in First Corinthians, chapter 15. I have, under my hand and borrowed from the cathedral library, the most influential text in our language. It is Tyndale's 1534 translation of the New Testament, together with the variants of the first edition of 1525.

Recently I was speaking to American students in University College, Oxford, about old alumni of the university who had been important for the life of the United States – men like William Penn and John Wesley. I began, however, by withholding the most important name of all because I said it would be totally unknown to them. Certainly his name was long forgotten in the United States and even ignored in England. In the end I announced it as William Tyndale of Magdalen Hall, class of 1515.

Let me make a bold claim. Tyndale is the single most important influence on what is now the world language, bar none. You will say, 'But what about Shakespeare?' Yet, as a matter of fact, Shakespeare was not much heard, let alone read, by the majority of people in English-speaking countries up to the late nineteenth century. Even when his plays were performed they were truncated as to form and corrupt as to text. Tyndale, however, was both heard and read: heard by the illiterate, and by the late seventeenth and early eighteenth centuries, increasingly read. And that is because, as a reading of the Parable of the Prodigal Son shows, Tyndale is substantially the author of the Authorized Version (AV) published in 1611. Go through a few pages of St Matthew's gospel and it is clear that hundreds of phrases embedded in our daily speech are Tyndale's. 'Pearls before swine', 'was lost and is found', 'the salt of the earth', 'by their fruits', 'in the twinkling of an eye', 'O ye of little faith', 'Consider the lilies'; all of them Tyndale. Tyndale's stated ambitions as a translator were realized. First, as he died, he prayed, 'Lord, open the King of England's eyes'. They were opened, within four years. Second, as he lived, he prayed that the Bible might be known; 'by him that followeth the plough'. And it was so.

There is more to be said. Tyndale and the other Renaissance translators who followed him, because they reproduced the syntax of Hebrew and of Greek, but especially of Hebrew, created the syntax of modern English. A rabbi once said to me, 'If I recite a psalm to you in Hebrew, you should be able to recognize the text of the AV by the way it breathes'. The same is true, incidentally, of Cranmer's recreation of the marvellous music of mediaeval Latin. Read English sentences of the early sixteenth century and you will see how bulky they are and how apt to run out of control. The Renaissance translators, led by Tyndale, brought order and concision to our language. They also built in resonance and artful implication and play. Read the story of the temptation of Adam and Eve, and see how Tyndale implies theology by playful reiteration of the words 'Know' and 'Knowledge': 'And Adam knew Eve' ... 'they knew that they were naked'.

Here I cannot resist a polemical paragraph. If what Tyndale wrote in 1525 is 70 per cent of the AV, then the AV was archaic from the moment of issue. The translators were not bothered about being archaic, nor for that matter were they bothered about literary English or something called everyday English. Rather they sought and found a form of English for speaking about the mystery of God. This is *not* at all to imply that we haven't needed contemporary versions of the Bible embodying the scholarship of four centuries. But it is to scotch the idea that there is an everyday English, let alone one which has been achieved by modern translations.

Perhaps one thing further should be added to take the measure of what we now commemorate. The Protestant nations of Europe, Wales, England, Germany and the rest, have created great literatures saturated in their classical renaissance translations. Indeed, their very birth coincided with the birth of the Bible in the vernacular. Tyndale did for England what Luther did for Germany, and indeed he plundered Luther to do it. That means that when you read (say) Ruskin's 'Unto this last' you are entering an echo-chamber of conscious and sub-conscious recollection. What is a film title like *Chariots of Fire* but the Second Book of Kings mediated through Blake's Jerusalem? What is the quotation on the label of Tate and Lyle's Golden Syrup but Samson's riddle to the Philistines in the Book of Judges: 'Out of the strong came forth sweetness'? What was John Edmonds' speech to the 1994 Labour Party Conference but an adaptation of the First Corinthians, chapter 13: 'And the greatest of these is full employment.'

Tyndale's life was brief. Born in 1494, he was strangled and burned in Vilvorde, Flanders on 6 October 1536, aged 42. Isaac Foot, father of Michael Foot, in the introduction to Tyndale's text says that 'he was in exile, a hunted man, with a price on his head, forced to hide from his enemies, who having burned his books were determined to burn him'. To give you the spirit of the man let me quote what he said when he met one of the envoys of the Low Countries outside the gates of Antwerp in 1531. 'Do you not know me? My name is Tyndale ... If for my pains therein taken, if for my poverty, if for my exile out of my natural country, and bitter absence from my friends, if for my hunger, my thirst, my cold, my great danger wherewith I am encompassed, and finally if for innumerable other hard and sharp fightings, which I endure ... ' *That* is his autobiography.

Why such sharp fightings, why so terrible a death? It is impossible now to imagine the terror felt by ecclesiastics in the 1530s in case 'him that followeth the plough' should also be able to follow the Word of God. Today, some Muslims threaten the life of Salman Rushdie on account of *Satanic Verses*; four and a half centuries ago Christians threatened and took the life of William Tyndale on account of giving them the Bible in English. No wonder Thomas Cranmer said in the late 1530s that if we wait for the bench of Bishops to authorize the Bible in English, we shall (I quote), 'wait until the day after doomsday'. Yet there was reason in their terror. Thomas More was horrified by the fact that Tyndale was able to translate the word, hitherto translated 'priest', first by the word 'senior' and then by the word 'elder'. Tyndale knew that there was no such thing as a word for word translation.

Translation is always interpretation and therefore full of danger. Look at Tyndale's own introduction to his New Testament entitled 'W T unto the Reader'. This is not just a manifesto of the New Learning of Erasmus and Colet but the vigorous polemic of the smallish Protestant minority in early Tudor England. It reminds us, if we care to read Eamon Duffy's *The Stripping of the Altars* that there is another side to the story and that England did not become fully Protestant until about 1580. But the polemic is superb. Tyndale's adversaries appear to him as the modern Pharisees. He addresses them with the vehemence of his Lord. They have locked up salvation and thrown away the key. They dispute 'thereof as sottelye as the popyshe doctours of dunces dark learning'.[1] But there is more than polemic. We hear the high trumpet tunes of reformed Christianity according to which repentance of the heart takes precedence over the priestly sacraments of penance. There is a world-shaking revolution here implied in the shift from a sacrament of penance to the inward circumcision of the heart. The individual standing before God and before His Word without intermediary took responsibility for his eternal salvation, through grace and through faith in the blood of Christ. *Sola fide, sola gratia, sola scriptura.* As William Tyndale put it, the heart of the matter is to be converted and 'to tourne to God with all the hert, to knowe his will and live according to his lawes and to be cured of oure corrupt nature with the oyle of his spirit and the wine of obedience to his doctrine'. Can we not hear in this the urgent cadences of the *Book of Common Prayer* inserting within the proper and priestly office of absolution the Protestant demand for a repentance of the heart? 'He pardoneth and absolveth all them that truly repent and unfeignedly believe his holy gospel.'

Alan Bennett's book *Writing Home* has an affectionate chapter on the *Book of Common Prayer* in which he says that Cranmer did not devise the Prayer Book or die a martyr's death in Oxford for the benefit of English prose. No more did Tyndale translate the Bible to found our language or create our inheritance and service the heritage industry. He founded our language only because he had something earnest and most urgent to say. The two things go together. Form and content are not divided. What people remember is what is memorable. The urgency of the message informs its delivery. And the message of Tyndale was the mystery of God and the issues of life and death. It is that which alone creates the exultant rhythm of the English Bible. Listen to it again as when first created near Little Sodbury in the quiet countryside of Gloucestershire before it spread to the ends of the earth.

> Behold, I shewe you a mystery. We shall not all slepe; but we shall all be changed, and that in a moment, and in the twinclinge of an eye, at the sounde of the last trompe. For the trompe shall blowe, and the deed shall ryse incorruptible, and we shall be chaunged. For this corruptible must put on incorruptibilite; and this mortal must put on immortalite.
>
> When this corruptible hath put on incorruptibilite, and this mortall hath put on immortalite; then shalbe be brought to passe the sayinge that is written. Deeth is consumed in to victory. Deeth where is they stynge? Hell where is thy victory? The stynge of deeth is synne; and the strength of synne is the lawe. But thankes be vnto God, which hath geven vs victory, thorow oure Lorde Jesus Christ.

Note

1 A reference presumably to Duns Scotus (hence 'Dunce') who was known as the Subtle Doctor, i.e. a pedant not a fool. I wish to acknowledge considerable reliance in the above, not only on Isaac Foot's Introduction to Tyndale's Bible, but also on Gerald Hammond and George Steiner on issues of text and translation.

Rededication of the House: St Peter's, Old Woking, 1995

Thou hast said my name shall be there.

1 Kings, chapter 5, verse 5.

You also, as lively stones, are built up a spiritual house and holy priesthood to offer up spiritual sacrifices acceptable to God by Jesus Christ.

First Epistle of Peter, chapter 2, verse 5.

The first text comes from the prayer offered by Solomon at the consecration of the Temple. God, he says, does not depend upon being housed. The One who is from everlasting to everlasting is not dependent on the creations of time. The infinite and universal God cannot be contained by creation itself, much less by a human shelter. Nevertheless, that shelter is the place designated for worship: special to divine purposes. It is where prayer has been made without cessation. And above all, says King Solomon, it is where the holy name is uttered and made known. 'My name shall be there.' To pronounce God's name here is not just to make a passing reference to an idea but to unveil a presence. We do not pray to God without first uttering the name – 'Our *Father*, which art in heaven, hallowed be thy *name*.'

Prayer is invocation, which literally means 'naming', a calling upon and a calling up of all that He is. So this is the place where God is named, the Lord of Hosts, the King of Glory, the Fountain of Goodness, the Author of Peace and the Lover of Concord. That is what the Temple meant three millennia ago and what it means in this quiet corner by the River Wey. The Being whom we worship – beyond image, or formula, or space and time – can become specially manifest to us as we enter the sanctuary of His name and prayerfully invite His gracious presence. The Lord is here.

The second text offers a contrast but not, I think, a contradiction. I would say that in a profound sense it is evangelical. It is not concerned with the sanctuary or with any earthly location where God is named and invoked. Nor is it concerned with those who carry out sacred duties and offer prayer for the people. Rather it sees the human spirit as a kind of inward chamber in which we receive a most glorious Lord. A temple made with hands centring the community becomes an inner temple centring the individual soul. The visible priesthood merges into the invisible sacrifice made by a contrite heart. And so there is both the holy place where God is named by his servants; and there is the inner temple where our spirit makes the offering of the heart. God has tangible signs, of which this church is one, with its visible gifts of bread and of wine, and He is intangible peace and love and joy and wonder and fulfilment.

And that then is the twofold theme given by our texts. I would call it place and person; physical stone and lively stone; tangible sign and intangible spirit. Before I look at each in turn I would like to suggest that both are precarious; and I have a special affection for that word 'precarious' because it literally means 'standing in the need of prayer'. Perhaps as you came in you realized just how precarious, just how 'standing in the need of prayer' are the supporting beams in the tower. This house stands but it stands in need of a great deal of prayer, and of care, and of attention. And that is costly. The precarious is costly. And the lively stones of this spiritual house are also precarious. Each spirit here stands in need of prayer, and care, and attention. We all of us whether explicitly Christian or just serious people, must watch over ourselves and others with care. Are we, are they, on the verge of breakdown? Has the frail house of the spirit begun to cave in? Ruin can attend the spirit, and it can so easily happen if nobody cares or if we simply fear to enquire. Or have we perhaps been eaten away inside for years, dried out even beyond our own tears? We are all of us precarious creatures needing renewal. That too is costly. Conversion and redemption are costly.

Let me say something about this place, about these physical stones and their story. Probably some kind of sacred spot existed here by the stream among these meadows and forests long before the coming of Christianity. Just for a moment forget the Christian presence and imagine the first breaking of the good news in 'Wok's Inge', the homestead by the Wey of the people led by Wok. Probably the message was brought by monks from Peterborough. And very likely Wok's people, or their descendants, built a prayer house as the old gods were slowly relegated and the older rites of sun and moon, of war and fertility half forgotten. Maybe there have been thirteen centuries of prayer and praise on this site. And certainly large parts of this church have been here for nine of those centuries. So what we see today is the result of constant repair, and addition, and replacement, and reconstruction generation after generation. When somebody installed this pulpit and added that gallery in the reign of James I, there had already been half a millennium of deterioration and restoration.

Churches resemble human bodies, identifiable, with a certain character over time, but renewed every few years. And perhaps you can even imagine the shifting populations of the previous twenty-eight generations and their replacement as they lived their lives around this little nucleus and its scattered farmsteads in the shadow of great houses still here and stately palaces long vanished into thin air. The new replaced the old in a steady rhythm of birth and marriage and death. First entrance in, growth, occupancy, departure. And then that perpetual cycle was disturbed by an industrial revolution beginning in England, altering the face of the whole earth and creating among myriad other things, the new Woking we know today. New Woking is linked to the railway age, to the movement of cemeteries out of London to healthy pinewoods, to the spread of suburbs and to the building of new estates. And the Victorians who made New Woking did a great deal to preserve an older England – sometimes with more zeal than sensitivity – but they did it, including the restoration of thousands of parish churches, among them this.

And now they, too, are history, no longer an oral recollection of even our grandparents, but figures locked in history books. The church they restored has once again suffered change and decay and we have asked ourselves with deepening anxiety questions which they first framed. 'Is this new world where man visits the moon, and revises even his own genetic programme, one destined to be faith-less?

Are we humans wired-up facsimiles merely imagining soul, and spirit, and if so, why has a facsimile acquired so odd an imagination and framed so curious a question? Is the ancient cycle of restoration and deterioration entering a terminal phase or – and this depends on us – are things thrown down, once again being raised up?'

And that debate cannot be opened here, but my own answer would be that faithlessness is an oddity of the Europe that first invented modernity. The fragmentations we have undergone under the extraordinary accelerations of history will prelude and do prelude a recovery. And, of course, the returning 'sea of faith' never comes back up precisely the same channels but it will, I believe, bear a recognizable sign, an historic identity, a reference back to divine origins. And that depends on the linkage of the physical stones of this sanctuary with the lively stones of the spirit. We have to become attentive to the spirit.

What is it to be attentive to the spirit? It is, I think, to become knowledgeable about the precarious position we are in, how much we stand in the need of prayer. That is the first act of attention to the spirit. And the second act is to scrutinize our lives to see what things truly matter in them. Where lie our worst fears and our best hopes? And it is at that point that we are ready for vision and for revision or (if you prefer an older language) prepared for conversion and redemption. We allow a deeper self to emerge, less at the mercy of surface changes and chances, more attuned to the resources of spiritual refreshment and to those powers which redress and redeem and recover. And what we recover is wonder, wonder at creation, its detail and its splendour, and responsiveness to grace and to love – above all to the grace and the love manifested for us, to us, in Christ Jesus. To be attentive to the Spirit is to become hospitable to divine grace and allow it free passage. In Christ's own words (the words of the cornerstone of the faith) it is to 'seek first the Kingdom of God'. The rest, he promised, will follow.

Sacred Place and Secular Government:[1] 900th Anniversary, Winchester Cathedral, 1993

> Lord God of Israel, there is no God like thee, in heaven above or on earth beneath, who keepest covenant and mercy with thy servants that walk before thee with all their heart.
>
> First Book of Kings, chapter 8, verse 23.

> He that loveth his brother abideth in the light.
>
> First Epistle of John, chapter 2, verse 10.

I see these two lessons as complementary. The Old Testament lesson is a prayer for the people by Solomon as their head of state on the occasion of the consecration of the Temple. It invokes and surveys the public good, item by item. The public good includes protection against the assaults of enemies and national disasters, the just regulation of relationships between neighbours, a proper respect for the stranger within the gates, and due reverence for divine laws and statutes. The New Testament lesson is different. It goes beyond the state of the nation to the state of the heart. John, as a father-in-God, speaks to his children-in-Christ of personal goodness and brotherly love.

These two lessons are complementary because they represent the twin aspects of our civil society and our common weal: on the one side, the good health of the body politic, on the other side the goodwill and good heart of our personal relationships. We have external agencies governing our common life as citizens; we have inward dispositions and affections governing our mutual care for each other as persons.

Nothing could be more fundamental than these twin aspects and to hear of them once again through ancient scripture is to remind ourselves on the verge of a third millennium how long and deep are the taproots of our civilization. We go back over millennia to the great codes of the ancient world for our understanding of public good; and we reach back to Christian and other explorations of the internal forum of the soul for our understanding of personal probity, good faith and integrity. Earlier this year, I stood on the Mount of the Beatitudes overlooking the northern shore of Galilee and read these words: 'Blessed are the poor', 'Blessed are the merciful', 'Blessed are the peacemakers', 'Blessed are they that hunger and thirst after righteousness.' As I read, people from all nations were passing quietly by. A young Frenchwoman turned to me, and said: 'It is central. There is nothing more central.' We were standing beyond any possibility of forgetting on the meridian line of the moral world.

Nor can the terms of our contemporary political debate in England forget these deep foundations of what we mean by public good, and of our personal concern one for another. I would mention only Tony Blair, Alan Beith and Douglas Hurd among politicians whose concern happens to be directly Christian. The stress varies, of course, as between law and order, or equity and welfare, in the public space; and as between the freedom needed to help create a self and the moral education and admonition required to foster goodwill, good faith and honest intent in the individual citizen. But everyone recognizes that total state control breeds impersonality and corruption; and everyone recognizes that gross inequity drains the moral authority of our society and eats away at the resources of goodwill. I have a sense at the present time that employment-led changes, such as casualization, part-time working, very low pay, the loss of any secure prospects, the uselessness of many skills, and all the consequences that follow for expectations about homes and housing, or for attitudes towards migrants, are leading to a massive corrosion of the moral authority of government and of the sources of meaning and responsibility and purpose in millions of individual lives. In such a situation, we need both an intelligent understanding of rapid social change, especially of what we are learning to call the flexible labour market, and a decisive rethinking in the light of the moral foundations.

Because we are now celebrating the 900th anniversary of the consecration of this holy house, I want to say something about the relevance of its message to that agenda, to a recall to the foundations. To some, the cathedral is simply a sermon in stone about continuity and durability. There has been witness made here from the moment of the first sacred settlement to the day Philip of Spain and Mary Tudor were married a few feet from where I stand, to the moment Jane Austen was buried a few feet from where you sit, and then on, up to the 13th of June 1993. The cathedral stands. But what does it stand for?

The cathedral stands for a transcendent possibility glimpsed through our mundane preoccupations, without which law is only social control, and government – national or local – simply the utilitarian administration of things. It also stands for the idea of a centre, for human life as something that should be centred. Of course, no one doubts that historically this spot has been the physical centre of the wide region of which you are the honoured representatives. Here is a bower in the hills, a break through which a river runs, where the ancient highways met, where markets grew, power was established and abused, law dispensed and counsel taken. This is – still – the physical, spatial heartland of an ancient kingdom, never quite forgotten. But it also claims to be, with every other consecrated spot, the heartland of a spiritual kingdom. However frail, however marooned and bypassed, here is a fellowship of music and of silence, where prayer is offered and the greatest story told. Where else is this lamp to be lit, this truth guarded, and this witness maintained?

So *what* prayer is continued here, *what* story told? Prayer spreads our life before God, or, if you prefer another language, it stands in profound seriousness and self-scrutiny before the sources and resources of our life and being. Prayer recollects what continues worthy of our respect, enquires what now should engage our humane concern, and envisions what better future we might pursue. To pray is to cease for a moment from the assertion of rightness and righteousness somehow demanded by the disciplines of everyday life and of politics to allow other things to announce a presence: regret, self-questioning, sorrow that past actions might have been other and better than they were. In prayer our urgent concerns become momentary in the long durance of history and God's good time.

And what story is told? Every individual, every people, needs a narrative of the perilous passage through time. I have a fear this people has half lost the thread of the narrative. It has too little sense that all education has to do with a partnership in perfection over time, conveyed in a purposeful tale. Only to teach skills, however essential, is to invite a loss of purpose in pure technique; only to encourage self-expression is to give too much place to a pursuit of personal pleasure and greedy profit, and a jostling of unsatisfied selves. We need a good story, a moral landscape of admonition and promise, for people who have sustained a bad Fall, but nevertheless seek a better city; and en route that story should tell them who is their neighbour, how to find a way home after prodigal expenditure in a waste land, and how to recognize a pearl of great price when they see it. The story turns on the most basic and simplest principle of all, in the words of John 'He that loveth his brother abideth in the light'.

Note

1 Visit of the county government of Hampshire.

Remembrance of Things Past: Guildford Cathedral, November 1989

Man does not live by bread alone.
(My text is taken from Mr Gennady Gerasimov, Russian Foreign Office spokesman, commenting on the collapse of the Berlin Wall.)

On Remembrance Sunday central London lay almost immobile under the November sun. The noble spaces of Whitehall were full of plangent and sombre sounds recollecting the griefs of seventy-five years since 1914. Every year we make the memorial of unnumbered deaths and woundings, and remember that this has been the century of total war. At the same time, last Sunday in central Berlin a concrete reminder of grief and waste and division was being finally torn down and resolutely forgotten. People leapt over the wall shouting 'The Wall is dead'.

Perhaps the seventy-five years are very nearly at an end. At least within our particular stream of history a terrible past seems suddenly receding at speed, and we feel tempted to say 'Look we have come through' or 'Everyone suddenly burst out singing' or even 'Bliss was it in that dawn to be alive'. Of course, those are the words of people at other moments of hope, in 1789 and 1918, who were soon bitterly disillusioned. Yet the things we see are on the margin of miracle. There have been televized pictures of President Weizäcker speaking at the Reconciliation Church in Berlin and a burst of ecstatic music from the choir reminding us of all the grave constancies never obliterated by the tanks and meathooks. At Mass in German-speaking Polish Silesia, Chancellor Kohl clasped the hands of the Polish Prime Minister in a gesture of permanent reconciliation. At Vilnius in Lithuania the cathedral is once again a house of prayer after decades as a museum or storehouse. We can only half imagine what it meant for the aged Archbishop once more to prostrate himself trembling before the altar in the company of tens of thousands of his fellow countrymen. *Introibo ad altare Dei.* I will go in unto the altar of God.

It is even possible in our sub-continent, if not in Peking or San Salvador, that we are watching the emergence of gentler ways both of governance and of protest. In 1968 an apprentice pastor, Jan Palach, felt he had to burn himself to death in response to the armed seizure of Prague. Now it seems that people can express their desire for better things, for bread and more than bread, by peaceful walks and demonstrations of candle power up to their Parliament Buildings in Budapest, into the squares and churches of Leipzig, even around the walls of the Lubianka Prison. It is almost as if Palm Sunday is enough: crucifixion for the moment suspended.

And yet we all realize that the fall of Stalin's brutalism and the breakdown of just one version of apartheid is not some 'end to history'. Today's promise includes threat. We need not suppose it's going to be Horizon Tours and Health Foods from now on. In the same breath as we give thanks for the tenacity of faith and identity in Lithuania or Georgia or the Ukraine, we know that what has been lifeblood for one people is easily deadly poison for others. People inherit adjacent lands or even share them whose loyalties, historic memories and foundation myths are worlds apart or even militantly opposed. In places where the great confessional borders run in jagged faults from Londonderry to Lebanon and Kosovo to Azerbaijan, it is still possible for the marvellous resources of faith and language and historic memory to be pitted against each other in deadly enmity. Just because we hold so tenaciously to the great codes which make life intelligible and just because we sink roots so deep in mother country and father land, terror and repression easily follow. The things which stabilize and frame us and make us resourceful are deep-dyed in moral ambiguity. So I want, in the remaining time, to look first at these morally ambiguous resources present in the stirring of peoples and recovery of roots, and then to touch on those special resources which seem to be good almost beyond ambiguity.

Almost all peoples imagine themselves 'special' in what they take to be the providence of history. They all devise some idealization of their historic past and present purpose: Poland to be martyred, France to be a nursery of civilized arts; Norway to reverence nature and pursue peace, Switzerland to be Second Eden and dispense aid, England to be a 'right little tight little island', and defend liberty. These images are a tribute paid by power to virtue and they can even lure us to embody them. They are also a sort of happy imitation of the fraternity of Christ's Church. Yet there is simultaneously a blasphemous parody of the Kingdom of God, in the Reich which lasts a thousand years, and in the prayer for God to make Britain mightier yet. The images on the reverse side of the national coin are of brutal inflation: the expulsion of the stranger and the annihilation of 'the other'. One moment one side of the coin is uppermost, the next moment the other, and we all slide imperceptibly from building Jerusalem 'in England's green and pleasant land' to 'Land of Hope and Glory'.

Where then is the unambiguous good and how do we locate Jerusalem which is the mother of us all and not – like Jerusalem today – the hub of hatred? For myself I had almost my first intimation of this alternative citizenship just after the war when I hitch-hiked to an international youth gathering on the Lorelei Rock 400 feet above the Rhine. After much lecturing on liberty and unity we came together for morning service in an open-air amphitheatre once used for Nazi rallies. I remember only the Lord's Prayer which we spoke together in several languages, and the way the sinister word 'Reich' touched for a moment against the good word 'Kingdom'. That moment initiated me into a universality in which all the walls and partitions were down.

I also find an – almost – unambiguous good in peaceful walking and demonstration. I do not mean that I approve of all the demonstrations, but I do believe there are peaceable processions which are 'not far from the Kingdom'. Many of them in Europe today are made up of people who bear Christian signs, above all candles. We see these processions and these signs and I think we recognize an *attempt to reclaim the city*, a kind of Palm Sunday. When two million people link arms all along the borders of the Baltic Republics it is not entirely unambiguous, but the ringing of all the church bells at the same time is a good and unthreatening sign. When the vast crowds gathering in Leipzig fill up the Nicholas Church and all the other central churches they are seeking out sacred and inviolate space above all the claims of profane jurisdiction and arbitrary power. This, they say, is where the grave constancies are celebrated and recollected.

The final location of the inviolate Kingdom and of the unambiguous good is in our selves; the *inner* forum which remains when the outer forum is occupied. There is a self which can still hold the imprint of God's own image whatever lies and imprisonment and violence can do. I encountered it for myself in 1988, when I met the Russian poet, Irina Ratushinskaya. Before even knowing who she was I realized that here was somebody 'full of grace'.

In 1982, Irina Ratushinskaya was sentenced to twelve years' imprisonment and internal exile for writing poetry which pitted her truth against what the state called its 'reality'. As she was taken away by train into a special prison called Small Zone she appeared to be quite alone. But she was not quite alone, because she knew that she was upheld in a union of love, concern and prayer. The day after she was released, 10 October 1986, by order of Mikhail Gorbachev, she wrote in her poem 'Believe me' that she and all the others incarcerated could not have passed through everything except for knowing that friends were 'petitioning the Lord' on their behalf.

You are right excellent Mr Gerasimov.

'Man does not live by bread alone – but by every word which comes out of the mouth of God.'

War, Peace and Remembrance: AD 2000

I will gather all nations and tongues.

Isaiah, chapter 66, verse 18.

But the Jerusalem above is free, and the mother of us all.

St Paul's Epistle to the Galatians, chapter 4, verse 21.

I should explain that this is an experiment. I have been asked to combine my roles as theologian and sociologist in trying to link sociological and Christian approaches to violence and war, as well as conflicts between peoples, and conflicts between faiths – which often amount to the same thing.

The two approaches are very different. Christianity has a *vision* of all peoples gathered together at a shared table, whereas sociology *analyses* why tribes always behave tribally. Christians *believe* some kind of revolution was set in motion two millennia ago, but *observation* shows that the age-old order of power and violence, enmity and separation has never been shaken, and that Christianity itself gradually found it politic to collude with empire, making the cross a sign of power as well as a powerful sign of salvation. And the problem arises not because power is wrong in itself, since it is necessary both for justice and peace, but because politics does not respond to the initiatives of love and reconciliation.

The answers to that problem are mainly sociological though ethologists and biogeneticists believe they have explanations in terms of the 'territorial animal' and assisting the survival of one's own gene pool. The central question I ask as a sociologist has to be: how does the unarmed and borderless Kingdom of God infiltrate a political order based on territory and arms, 'Us' and 'Them', and power and interest?

My strategy is to focus on Jerusalem, because it throws the question into dramatic relief. The very name Jerusalem means peace and unity, yet its history has so often been one of war and division. All three of its warring faiths, Jewish, Christian and Muslim, have proclaimed one God and one humanity, and pronounced the word of peace: *Pax*, *shalom*, *salaam*. Yet they have divided the city between them, turning Jerusalem into a Babylon of mutual incomprehension. That still does not mean we are completely locked in endless conflict with no hope of relief. New visions create new horizons and in the Bible we can trace how that comes about. We have always to deal with Nehemiah's vision of Jerusalem as the prized citadel of an exclusive ethnic faith, but in Isaiah there is also an open city offering its light to the gentiles, and in St John the Divine Jerusalem becomes the spiritual sign of the peaceable kingdom.

Perhaps in an experimental address I can make three controversial statements. First of all, I do not believe, in spite of the Armenian, Jewish and other holocausts, and the two world wars, that the last century was unique in the terrible tally of human suffering. The 'abomination of desolation' is a constant possibility. Gregory

Baum, the Jewish Catholic theologian once asked me how I had altered my theology in response to twentieth-century horror and I answered not at all, because any serious theology, like any serious sociology, has to begin with the high places laid waste and the people carried away.

Second, I do not believe that any nation can be stained by collective guilt to the second or third generation. Though people habitually refer to what 'we' or 'they' once did amiss, that is only a manner of speaking. We sin in Adam, as a flawed species, and in what we personally have done or left undone, but no matter what some people may have perpetrated in time past *we* do not carry a tribal taint. The girl born yesterday in Dresden bears no responsibility for Auschwitz, and the boy born yesterday in Bristol bears no responsibility for the bombing of Dresden, or for the Bristol slave trade. So when we speak of the need for political apology, contrition and forgiveness, we have to be very careful about who is forgiving whom for what, when.

My last provocation is actually the key to what follows. Christ told Pilate his kingdom was 'not of this world' which means the prayer 'Thy kingdom come' can never be realized as some kind of political *order*, though it carries political implications. Heaven lies about us and within us as faith, hope and charity, and we discover it 'at hand' in every sign of healing, offering, reconciliation and acceptance. But the political world still works by the rules of power and violence; and the corruptible regimes of the old gods are never publicly overthrown. At the same time they are undermined in ways Jesus foresaw by the silent leaven and the seed. Heaven's kingdom comes through a wild seed cast abroad, germinating far from the hand that scatters it, or the Church which carries it – still. The Christian education of the emotions is so often extra-mural, which means the Church will be judged by its own standards.

What then of the sociological account of war, division and enslavement? Well, the power, the glory, the native territory, its wealth, honour and shame, would provide a good start, but space and time allows only one strand of the argument, which I pick out because it really does allow me to relate sociological and Christian understandings. It concerns the stories tribes and nations tell of their origins and destinies, sufferings and triumphs, exiles and returns, martyrs and heroes. When we look at these stories we find at their heart binding covenants sealed in the blood of those who died that others might live, and we find perpetual memorials of their precious deaths. And, as such stories are told, a nation becomes like a Church, solemnly unified in a community of remembrance and hope.

And yet what brings people together under the sign of a good 'Us' easily divides people from a sinister 'Them', because the stories are idealized and neglect the dark side of the account. Think only of what Serbs tell the world about their martyrdom, exile and displacement, and the way that reinforces enmity and division between Serbs, believing themselves entitled to possess again their promised land, and the people now living in it.

Why am I using these Biblical echoes and phrases? Because I want to bring out both the powerful resemblances between national epics and the Bible story, and the way Christian nations have used scripture as their own script. There is a powerful resemblance between us and the Jews when we grieve at our own Wailing Wall and remember every November how the sea stood between us and Pharaoh, with his chariots, and the captains of his host. As for Scripture reused as a tribal script we remember how many nations have cast themselves as New Israel and their heroes and kings as Moses or Josiah, David or Solomon. But again the dark side is left out. Those so proud to remember their liberation from the Egyptians forget how they in turn have held peoples captive, or carried out their own ethnic cleansing. All nations trumpet the better half of their story, forgetting that what gave them a giant's strength to stand up also gave them a giant's strength to put down.

So then what we see in the Bible as the story of stories is a profound encapsulation of all this: the ideal and idealized hopes, and the frustrations en route, and the half-hidden dark realities: an Exodus from oppression, a Great Trek through the wilderness, and then arrival in a promised land, with divine authorization for ethnic cleansing. Yet the Bible also amplifies its vision all the way from the crossing of the Red Sea to the arrival of a New Jerusalem. Once the exclusive boundaries designed to ensure the survival of a people are in place, we see a new vision emerging which goes beyond them. Those who obey that vision move from special privilege to special responsibility, from keeping themselves apart to welcoming the stranger within the gate, from the multiplication of Abraham's physical seed to the scattering abroad of a spiritual seed, from a Jerusalem jealously guarded as the citadel of an ethnic faith with a divine land grant, to new Jerusalems which offer a light to the Gentiles and envisage a free city in the spirit, the 'mother of us all'.

So we are back to my initial question. Given the political order can be ameliorated but not overthrown what advent may we expect for the heavenly Jerusalem? Again the answer has to be: in the same way as the kingdom of which it is the capital. It is known in the leaven and the wild seed cast abroad. Though Christian faith makes its treaties with the political order, and sometimes fruitfully in the making of the Christian city, it also infiltrates the hope of an open spiritual concourse where all may enjoy mutual understanding. Babylon is overturned in the common speech of Pentecost. The veiled vision of love incarnate in word, sacrament and broadcast seed works a subtle subversion, putting about the rumour that the blood-soaked city of 'Babylon the great is fallen'.

When the Lord himself came to his last Passover and recited the story of liberation from the hosts of Egypt, he radically transformed its meaning. This was a covenant sealed in his own body and blood to break down the enmity and the separation so that all might come in and sit down at the supper. Here was the New Testament of the unarmed, borderless kingdom. And with that the local temple began to dissolve into the mystical body of Christ present in all times and places, and the physical Jerusalem became the spiritual space of a free city 'builded here', there and everywhere for 'all nations, tribes and tongues'.

The Meaning of a Cathedral: Guildford, 1993

This is none other but the House of God, and this is the gate of heaven.
Genesis, chapter 28, verse 17.

Human beings are odd animals. So far as they can they dispose of their dead with care, as if something more mysterious were involved than the disposal of inanimate matter. They laugh, which even dogs and horses don't do. They sit listening to air vibrating through pipes. They memorialize and imagine alternative futures, including immortality. They conceive of perfection and try to flesh it out. They condense meaning in sign and gesture.

Human beings enact, re-enact, and they process in patterns, with gravity and composure, and in silence. Speaking comes on cue, passing from voice to voice. Human beings can sing in chorus, each part adjusting continuously to all the others. They make obeisance with knees, or hands or head, or all together. Nearly all these pecularities are present in this marvellous building, except laughter. This place is serious. We took on seriousness as we crossed the threshold. We became inwardly attentive. We reduced eye contact and mutual recognition to a minimum to allow room for inwardness. We became still for God to be God.

This place, where God is God, is common land inviting anyone to walk on it, since God belongs to everybody. His door is always open. Approach Lincoln on its mound or St Mark's, Venice, in its square, and vast portals invite you in solely as a member of the species with tears and fears, joys and hopes. No other place in the city is set aside for everybody. And yet it is 'set aside'. A cathedral is set apart as holy, as inviolate, because here the past is stored, the dead received and honoured, the living blessed, the great codes held up, the sinful released, and sacrifice offered. Our understanding of the resplendent powers of good is centred here. Here the transcendent life of order confronts the chaotic order of our life. 'Take off thy shoes from off thy feet, for the place whereon thou standest is holy ground.'

Once I stood on Waterloo Bridge, looking towards St Paul's Cathedral, and remembering a comment of one of my academic colleagues: 'That is the only building in the city that has any meaning.' On the face of it, the remark is absurd, so I did a little five-finger sociological exercise to tease it out. I began with the National Westminster Bank, then the tallest building in the City, then the Law Courts, and then the University, just to my left.

The Bank is for the storage of material wealth. It has no interest in spiritual wealth. Try banking generosity and you will find it attracts no interest at all. A bank does not engage in solemn meditation. It has files, but no rites of recollection.

A law court embodies the Great Code on which any civilization must rest. But I have yet to meet the lawyer who says: 'O Lord, how pleasant are thy statutes; I meditate upon them day and night.' Of course, you can confess in a law court, but normally under duress. At best, you will be treated leniently. No lawyer advises you: 'If you confess your sins he is faithful and just to forgive you your sins.' Law, yes; grace, no. Go to the law courts (or the bank) and they will ask: 'What is your business?' It is no good replying: 'I am overwhelmed with grief', or 'I have just been surprised by joy.'

A university is rather different, which is why universities are sometimes close to cathedrals. It offers an open space for open enquiry. But if you say to university teachers: 'I am overwhelmed by grief', or, 'I have just been surprised by joy' they will reply: 'What a fascinating piece of data for the peak experience project' or, 'Perhaps a counsellor might help.' A university is a temple of truth but not of grace. Truth, yes; grace, no. Its Word never becomes ordinary human flesh, never offers itself up, never proclaims, 'Come unto me all ye that are heavy laden', or, 'In me your joy shall be full.'

But, some will say, this visual reading of the City as a kind of public profile for diverse purposes, coming to a high point in a central temple of humane and redemptive purpose, is not so easy for truly modern cities like New York or Chicago, or Hong Kong or Sydney. Such places are vertical concentrations where profane temples are dedicated solely to Mammon: Chase Manhattan, First City Bank. The various churches and cathedrals of a pluralistic society merely nestle at the bottom of canyons. Though the diversity of public purposes remains, the profile is drastically altered; or else we see, as at Strasbourg, an old city plainly beleaguered by the proximity of a new.

I, for one, do not accept this means the demise of the ancient idea of a cathedral, but notice that from this point on I am going to be contentious and have to ask pardon of colleagues who may disagree. Let me cite two modern parables. In Montreal a business consortium coveted the central site of the Anglican Cathedral. There was a civic struggle which, in the end, was resolved by the consortium building an enormous shopping mall *under* the Cathedral in gay modern Gothic. As you emerge from the mall, the shapes and colours of the Cathedral are brilliantly picked up and reflected in the glass tiles of the surrounding skyscrapers. The other parable is Liverpool after the Hillsborough football disaster. Thousands made their way first to the Catholic Cathedral for requiem mass and then later to the Anglican Cathedral for a memorial service, where the choir sang 'You'll never walk alone'. There have been similar events here ... such as the Service of Thanksgiving for British Airways as hostages were released in the Gulf War. Can we remember the dead, bless the living and renew sacrifices in Barclays, Mitsubishi or Chase Manhattan? Can we give thanks in the banks?

What then *is* the place of the cathedral as distinct from any other church, and apart from being the seat of an overseer of Christian souls? Being a centre and a focus requires a shift of scale: placing, spaciousness, dignity, height. Once purpose and scale are properly matched, worship undergoes a sea change. You have only three options: formality, pseudo-intimacy, or demagoguery. I believe, Cathedral worship has to be comely, grave and courteous. It is sacred theatre, suspending the casual and the chatty to unfold the mystery of redemption. We become aligned with a drama, not as individuals but as a people looking and facing east to Jerusalem and the dawn of the Sun of Righteousness. When we assemble in a cathedral we are a people, acknowledging dual citizenship: in the birthright community of place and history, and in the universal company of the Church.

I can only convey that dual citizenship in a final example. I take it from Helsinki, one of the most secular capitals in the world and a pioneer of modern architecture. The city now regularly invites its citizens into the centre for a festal day and night. As darkness fell, tens of thousands gathered in the central square, facing the steep steps below the colonnade of the cathedral. The dome was caught in shifting columns of light. Finlandia was played. You could overhear a people, a city, communing with itself. We were a concourse in the agora, the forum, the outer court, the piazza, the plaza, the platz, the square, the Grand Place. We were in continuity with every tremulous approach to the Keeper of all Being over millennia. The Cathedral itself was completely jammed for what is known as the St Thomas Mass, for those who barely believe but are happy to stand on holy ground, overhearing the Gospel in peace and goodwill. The sweet kernel of all this was simply an act of serious offering: the redemptive gifts of God and the answering sacrifices of a lowly heart. In this the inward and personal and the outward and public came together and the people of God carried out a witness which suffused, as far as it might, the wider community. Archbishop Laud put it best in his plea for cherishing the ceremonies and ancient liturgy of the Church: 'It is true' (he said) 'the inward worship of the heart is the true service of God; but the external worship of God in his Church is *the great witness to the world* that our heart stands right in that service to God'.

In Honour of St Cecilia: St Michael's, Cornhill

Come before his presence with a song.

Jubilate (Psalm 100, verse 1).

This is the feast of St Cecilia, patron saint of music. I would guess that the great period for celebrating her began about four hundred years ago, and in England some of the earliest celebrations were associated with Henry Purcell, one of them in the Stationers' Hall. At that time people were still influenced by a classical and Christian tradition for which music manifested the cosmic order over against the distracted atoms of primeval chaos.

From Harmony, from heavenly Harmony
This universal Frame began:
From Harmony to Harmony
Through all the compass of the notes it ran,
The diapason closing full in man.

Both Shakespeare and Milton would simply have assumed that in music we overhear the celestial mathematics and movements undergirding the universe. Even Addison who lived on the cusp of change when the singing spheres had been reduced to planets in trajectories believed they all shone and sang of their Creator in the ear of reason.

Of all the arts music has been the most intimate with faith. Some musicians, like Vivaldi and Liszt have been ordained, and divine worship is a partnership of priest and musician. Like most partnerships it has its inharmonious moments, as at Westminster Abbey, for example, when Handel vigorously declared he chose the words of the Coronation Anthems without clerical interference. Thomas Hardy's poem, 'The Choirmaster's Burial' set by Britten is a cameo of classic misunderstanding. The choirmaster wistfully wanted viols playing the tune 'Mount Ephraim' at his graveside, but:

'I think,' said the vicar, 'a read service quicker' …
'That old-fashioned way, Requires a fine day.'

But then at dead of next night an angelic band all in white alighted to sing and play 'the ancient stave by the choirmaster's grave'. Perhaps even more important is the tension of the good with the beautiful: how do we meet the just demands of Lazarus the beggar with his sores and also respond to music's resplendent echo of heaven?

The tension runs for centuries and from the earliest times. Is music a dangerous lilting seduction or an epiphany of the divine? St Augustine could not quite make up his mind, though in the joy that followed his baptism in Milan he wept as 'The sounds flowed in my ears and the truth distilled in my heart'. Even today ministers choose hymns for their words and congregations enjoy them for their tunes. For the minister the clarity of the message comes first and music is the handmaid or accompaniment.

Yet music is more than accompaniment because it deals in the subliminal and the sublime. Music sets the tone and through 'the channel of the ear' becomes the instrument of an almost sacramental transformation of how we see the world: not recreation but re-creation, making all things new. Nor is this power confined to serious music. When Sir Thomas Browne in the seventeenth century overheard popular music issuing from a tavern he confessed that still it has 'something of divinity in it'. The sanity of soldiers in the First World War whose nerves were shattered by the 'murderous anthems' of the guns revived their spirits with 'Who were you with last night?' When at last life and peace triumphed over death and destruction, 'everyone burst out singing'. Music is the sunburst of glory and primal joy.

> Music to hear, why hear'st thou music sadly?
> Sweets with sweets war not, joy delights in joy.
>
> To music bent is my retirèd mind.

When dumb with grief or speechless with joy we ring bells.

Let me count some of the ways music and faith resonate together. Both faith and music are rooted in discord and its resolution. As all movement in music turns on the alternation of the restless and the restful, including the arrest of silence, so the dynamic of faith turns on the alternation of God's absence and presence. If God were obviously and continuously present we could not begin to approach him. There would be no movement of faith.

Faith and music are both gift and practice. For faith there is the offer of free grace where nothing is required beyond an honest desire and goodness of heart. Yet faith is also repetition and learning how to wear the habit of virtue and to practise the presence of God. In music, too, there is the element of gift and, for some, of inspiration. Yet mastery comes only through the most exacting discipline of feeling and understanding. In practice and interpretation you must not seek your own or interpose your self but allow the other to be manifest through you: not self-expression but self lost in order to be found – Rosalyn Tureck's playing of Bach. The perfect is made known through attention and faithfulness.

When we consider faith or music it makes little sense to ask what they are for. The work of God we call worship and the revelatory works of the musical masters are justified in and for themselves. 'You *are* the music while the music lasts.' To come before God's presence with a song is to encounter the 'I am that I am'. In worship and music-making we are at our most serious and our most playful. 'We are the music-makers, we are the dreamers of dreams': so too were the prophets. Prelude, interlude, postlude, all have to do with playing. Perhaps only poetry is comparable because it is the profound play of words. To perform any of these miraculous arts we must 'learn to play' in and for the sake of the activity itself.

Most of our other activities are not like that. Here in the heart of 'the city' we find a kind of summation of human enterprise based on utility and exchange. The value of the goods – corn, drapes, fish, meat, stock, is expressed in price. That is precisely why in between the 'busy hum' of marts for buying and for selling you need sacred enclosures with spires and towers, bells and music, to express the goods 'without money and without price'. What is bought and sold exists in counterpoint with the priceless; in this space the cacophony of competitive bidding is matched by human voices in intimate consort one with another and by a prayer bidding us to other concerns. Here on the cornhill is a holy place for the celebration in word and music of what is justified in and for itself through that ceaseless overflow of sovereign grace and inspiration which is the 'real presence' of God.

Blessed Cecilia, appear in visions
To all musicians, appear and inspire:
Translated Daughter, come down and startle
Composing mortals with immortal fire.

Surprised by Joy: The Refreshment of Music

> And it came to pass, when the evil spirit from God was upon Saul, that David took an harp and played with his hand; so Saul was refreshed, and was well, and the evil spirit departed from him.
>
> 1 Samuel, chapter 16, verse 23.

Two groups of parents in Las Vegas are suing the group called Judas Priest for allegedly luring their sons to suicide with subliminal messages saying 'do it, do it, do it'. In England a person significantly and simply known as 'Abadan' is supposed to be a musical prophet of Satan. However, this 'Bad Un' doesn't deny it, which is unimpressive of him. It is difficult to think much of a devil-worshipper who hasn't the basic indecency to pretend to be 'Agoodan'.

What I find interesting about these accusations is that they only concern the verbal message and not the musical medium. Nobody has revived the age-old debate about the power of music itself for good or for ill. Yet among ancient Greeks, medieval Christians, and the thinkers of the Renaissance musical sounds themselves were regarded as capable either of devilish allurements or divine enchantment. There is an ancient tradition which affirms the power of music so to excite the affections and work upon the soul that a man or a woman is by turns amorous or destructive, soothed or jarred, called to dance or called to arms. You find that tradition finely expressed in Dryden's poem 'Alexander's Feast', set by Handel:

> Softly sweet in Lydian Measures.
> Soon he sooth'd his soul to Pleasures.

Whether David, the harpist-hero, used the Lydian measure is unrecorded, but he was one whose music soothed the soul and exorcised the disruptive spirit. Music was a kind of godly charm, using divine enchantment to expel malign influences.

So even though ancient speculation has supposed some musical modes and instruments to be diabolic or an invitation to lasciviousness, the overwhelming testament of music is to fellow-feeling, contentment and reconciliation. Even if there has to be a necessary collapse into the chaos of 'jarring sounds', the natural tendency is for notes to complement and complete each other. Music is, after all, about consonance, or things sounding together. The very word sinfonia signifies a coming together in mutual harmony.

In other words, music is a more trustworthy, gentler, kinder, more comely version of our world, full of heart's ease, consonance and natural virtue. It is a place where 'joy delights in joy'. And that is true not only of the highest reaches of serious music but of even the simplest invocations of harmony, rhythm or melody. They have a latent power to quieten and subdue. People are touched by the singing of a 'solitary highland lass', or by sounding brass, or by Edith Piaf, or massed voices across the field at Cardiff Arms Park, or a choirboy singing 'Jesus Christ the apple tree'. As I wrote this address, there were in some half-hidden gardens below me Italian students singing, 'Let it be, let it be; There will be an answer; let it be'. One of the most profound moments in the Promenade Concerts comes on the last night when a solitary string picks up the lament for the old sailor 'Tom Bowlin' and with the utmost purity and gentleness soars to a perfect cadence above the words 'And now he's gone aloft'. Thomas Browne said that even a casual hearing of 'vulgar tavern musick' struck in him a profound contemplation of the Creator.

What are we to make of this remark of Thomas Browne's, that music, even the sound of fiddling and jollity in the tavern, struck him with a profound contemplation of the Creator? It is a remark we have to take with great seriousness because people living in very varied times and circumstances have been 'struck' in exactly this manner. George Steiner in his book *Real Presences* speaks of the real presence in musical sound and can only conclude his argument about our god-haunted world by dropping words altogether, and saying '*Listen*'. Listen. Listen to Schubert's String Quintet. Emily Dickinson wrote:

> I've heard an organ talk sometimes
> In a cathedral aisle
> And understood no word it said
> Yet held my breath the while.

Wordlessness has superseded clear and distinct ideas and brought about a Pentecostal enlargement of the Spirit, enveloping men and all things in tongues of fire and holy charity.

Emily Dickinson has it right when she speaks of holding the breath, because we have been suspended by music, embraced and held up by it. The erratic pulse of the everyday world has encountered a more fundamental pulsation, more in accord with order. Whereas in mundane existence the things of time peter out or come to a dead end, in musical time they arrive at a perfect and satisfactory cadence. They come, so to speak, 'to the haven where they would be'. Day by day we are broken apart in meaningless pieces, where nothing fits together, where nothing is fitting, where there is no sense of the whole or wholeness, and where we can touch neither height nor depth. Yet in music things are rightly fitted together, the whole is fully present to us, and height and depth simultaneously encompassed. Whole movements are leaping probes to discover and uncover the incandescence at the centre, which burns but does not consume. It seems that throughout recorded time humankind has yearned for this inclusive untrammelled communication and found it in two opposite extremes, in music and mathematics, in notes and numbers. As the head of a music academy once put it to me, 'I am a musician to rediscover the meaning of Pentecost'.

Yet this is not without travail or cost. There is no serious recovery of the whole, or exploration of height and depth, or satisfactory arrival, which does not pass somewhere through heartbreak and desolation. The 'eternal note of sadness' creeps always in. Music, like faith, is a 'work', an Opus, and the greatest work is heartbreaking. There is a passage of arms somewhere in this work which deals in one blow after another, bereavement, abandonment, solitariness, desolation. And yet in music, by what alchemy we cannot guess, these terrors of love and death, are absorbed and transmuted. It is the power of music to re-present them to us, offer them again to us, in transfigured form. That is what makes music heartbreaking: this encounter with the whole burden of our sorrowful-ness and the ability to bear it and to carry it away. This is the way truly 'terrible beauty is born', by love in its encounter with death.

That makes of music something more than the happy expulsion of evil spirits by good spirits, or the optimism that supposes there will be an answer if you will only 'let it be'. Being is not enough. Music like faith has to pass through death and transfiguration. Music is the inclusion of sorrow within what is without question a jubilant testament of joy. And we have no idea why this is possible, why this reconciliation can be achieved at all, why there should be within the valley of ignorance and bafflement and defeat a luminous clearing where we are astonished, surprised and overwhelmed by joy. We merely know that it *is* and are thankful. The gift lies there, costly, precious and graceful, unexpected, in our hands.

Holy Matrimony I

Set me as a seal upon thine heart.

Song of Songs, chapter 8, verse 6.

Fiona and David,
There is no greater compliment one person can pay another than to risk and desire a lifetime spent in the other's company. It is a compliment paid in hope and faith as well as in love and truth. The ancient words 'I plight thee my troth' mean simply that in good faith I pledge you my truth whatever may befall. Those are large words for a difficult enterprise but love has never found any other language. Love promises without recourse to maybe or except or unless or until. It engages the future without condition.

Love also dares to engage the future in front of the whole world. Though it is so intimate and personal it wants everyone to know and recognize what has happened and specially seeks approval from those who matter most. If the circle of families is to be widened, sons and daughters welcomed and friends shared, the approval of loved ones counts a great deal. So marriage is not only an intimate pledge of good faith and truth, but a seal of approval. We all of us come here today to say we love and honour you both and are glad you have come together. Those closest to you of all show their pleasure and contentment in your pleasure and contentment.

This moment is an alignment of generations as well as an enlargement of the family circle. It is true that on this your own feast day you finally slip anchor in the previous generation and initiate your own. This is your time, your choice, your generation. But from another perspective you bring together the generations across time to subdue and annul it. The rivers of life which first sprang out of Eden are flowing now and we all have the privilege of celebrating a continuity of life from generation to generation. Maturity and old age have no consolations greater than the sight of children and children's children with their faces turned towards the future. Of course, there can also be deep sadness because so much is remembered as well as so much looked forward to. Griefs are recollected as well as joys anticipated and there are cherished pictures in our hearts. Nevertheless, this is a moment when your joy is full.

So let the hours and days to come be pure madrigal. Our earliest garden of delight, our first Eden, has never really been closed off and is there now for you to walk in. Whatever the season the seeds of love are sown in your own miraculous Rite of Spring. At the same time, you know well the long term fruits depend on watchful tending. They need the disciplines of love and the tender arts of marriage: how to turn time and work into servants not tyrants: how to give space for the other to grow: how to recognize the pressure points of unspoken hope or unspoken hurt.

I spoke just now of generations merging across time. The same is true of space. In most huddles of human habitation a prayer house is central, placing our most precious ventures in true perspective. Our separate trackways have come together from all points of the compass to meet in the sacred place. Here we not only recognize a contract but hallow a bond. We in the prayer house are all bonded together in common witness to the union of this man with this woman in the presence of God. Your relation one with another is set against the all-embracing vision of harmony we call the unity of God.

Fiona and David, I used that phrase 'all-embracing vision of harmony' of a purpose. Not only are you beginning to practise the exacting art of marriage but you are also talented in other arts, one of painting, one of music, to say nothing of cooking and chemistry. So I want now to trace some connections based on those talents by linking and comparing your arts of painting and music, and by letting them act as analogues and similitudes of the art of marriage and the science of God.

Leonardo da Vinci said that image and sound were the two perfect media, one for responding to the visible world, the other for responding to an invisible world. The links between them are clear even from our language. In both we speak of contrasts brought together in harmonious composition. In both we help create the transforming relationships we call revelation. Of course, nothing creative and nothing worthwhile is guaranteed. The good is always precarious. So in music there is false relation, in painting imaginative failure and disconnected chaos. But the shared vocabulary remains, of creation and revelation, unity and difference, juxtaposition and fusion. Whenever we bring things together in satisfying relations we are moved by love. Love moves all else, including yourselves, as painter, as musician, as human beings.

Take first painting, the art of making images. In the beginning our experience of the visible world of nature is unbounded, limited only by physical vision. Colour, shape, texture, delicate contrivance all wait invitingly for the operation of our inward eye to see how they might be brought together. Responding to this invitation you reveal the possibilities which lie there waiting in the profuse energies of nature. You frame them and create a new and unified field of relationships. What invites and moves you to do that is the outgoing spirit of intelligent love. According to Christian faith we respond lovingly and creatively to the invitation of the image because we are ourselves in the image of a loving Creator. Like him we are lovers and makers.

Music is very similar. Our ears pick up the endless profusion of sounds in nature, selectively attending to them and discovering the miraculous power of harmonious relation. To discover the sweet concord of sound with sound is to be drawn out of ourselves in pure enchantment. Then with our inward ear – paralleling our inward eye – we begin to order sounds in a time frame, until out of the genesis of a single note has sprung to birth new creation upon new creation. In every work of music movement complements rest and delight in difference mixes with pleasure in resolution. As in painting we imitate that loving conversation which is the inner life of God. Symphony simply means voices coming together. Those voices are nothing less than the common time shared by our human hearts and the intimate movement of that divine intelligent love which sustains the sun and all the other stars.

Fíona and David,
May the dove of peace descend with her olive leaf upon your ark,
granting you calm seas and prosperous voyaging;
And may goodness and mercy follow you all the days of your life:
In the name of the Father and of the Son and of the Holy Ghost. Amen.

Holy Matrimony II

> As the apple tree among the trees of the wood so is my beloved among the sons.
> Song of Songs, chapter 2, verse 3.

Clare and William,
For this most auspicious of occasions you offered me the very special privilege of giving your sermon. But you also instructed me to preach the Word, and by strong suggestions from what else you said, to preach the Word made flesh.

This, then, is a Christian sermon, and it has a Hebrew text from the Song of Songs, chapter 2, verse 3:

> As the apple tree among the trees of the wood
> So is my beloved among the sons.

There is, naturally, a supplementary and Christian sub-text, and I take it from the first of the three carols you chose to be sung later in the service. The words of that carol were written over two hundred years ago in New Hampshire by Joshua Smith. Like St Bernard, he saw in this ancient Hebrew poem of human love a mirror of the Lord's search for the soul. Growing out of the fount of human passion, Joshua Smith discerned the mysterious tree of life.

> The tree of life my soul has seen
> Laden with fruit and always green,
> The trees of nature fruitless be
> Compared with Christ the apple tree.

All those who love you know how strongly you desire to link the instinctual affections to sustained commitment. That is what a service of holy matrimony is about. But more than that this service is in every sense yours since you lovingly arranged each element, not just for decoration, but to frame in the most beautiful manner possible your own statement of commitment. Christian preachers, especially of the Reformation period, have often seen each of our lives as a text to be read by the world, but this text of yours incorporates the hope and faith of an intended life, together. So it is not just preacher and priest who read and 'take' the service. We all read it, and we all take it, to heart. As Beethoven said of his own very personal working of the text of the Mass:

> From the heart it has come, to the heart may it go.

So what is happening now can be seen as a kind of gentle and unobtrusive witness for whoever wishes to read: from you to us – but then also from us to you, because we are standing here in an act of solidarity, with you and for you. Your witness goes beyond the realm of law whereby you solemnly exchange vows and share every kind of good, to invoke the kind of relationships which are the ecology of the heavenly kingdom. Let me count the ways. You begin with an invitation to be awake and expect the coming of the Word; you continue with a psalm of approach to the sanctuary and a hymn to the holy spirit of charity. Then you place at the centre the human presence of the Word made flesh and you surround it with two joyful acclamations and a final hymn of adoration: O come, all ye faithful. There is, through all these choices, a vocabulary of expectation and gladness, unity and peace and plenteousness, ardour and yearning, illumination and praise, joy and exultation. And your three carols exhibit three guiding images: the apple tree, the birth of a child, and the bells of paradise.

I select one of these, the apple tree, as a special sign for your wedding. What shall I make of it?

The apple tree is one of the most daring and singular, intimate and luminous, of all the icons of our Saviour. It is luminous because, like the painting of Christ in the garden by Giovanni Bellini, it is lit from so many different sources of light. For example, it stands in the order of natural creation as a sign of fruitfulness. But, then, it stands in the human order as a sign of profound human affections. Finally, it stands on the ultimate horizon as a sign of Christ and of the divine love which is 'absolute sole lord of life and death'.

The Song of Songs has been milk and honey to the spiritual imagination of well over two millennia. God's people, the Jews, sing it on the Sabbath during Passover. The medieval saints and mystics browsed in its pastures, absorbing images of the rose of Sharon, the Lily of the Valley and the apple tree in the wood, as signs which unite the goods of earth with the treasures of heaven. In the figures of the lover and the loved they discerned a divine lover of souls searching day and night to bring us all under his banner of love.

It is probably my ignorance, but I have not encountered a theological working of 'Christ the apple tree', but I think I can guess how it should run. It would, surely, run in parallel with the mighty opposites of the Old Adam and the New as set up by St Paul. The Old Adam, Man inclusively and generically, is *de*generate. He has lost his way by overweening pride. He has been consumed by self-seeking for what Paul calls 'his own', or 'her own', which may be power or wealth or any other of the deep distractions of human life. That is why the Old Adam is debarred from the garden of true delights, condemned to be a thwarted, gross, unsatisfiable creature, like Alberic or Caliban, and wandering in a morose landscape of thorns and briars. The new Adam is *re*generate and his end is life not death, affirmation not destruction. He has found the stone which turns all else to gold and delivers to him all the treasures of heaven's peaceable kingdom. That miraculous stone is simply the grace of giving which seeks the good of the other in seeking the good of the self.

If now we set the apple tree within this polar contrast, then surely it must itself be contrasted with the fatal apple at the beginning of our human story. We can place the carol about Christ the Apple Tree against that other carol about Adam being in bondage for four millennia by grasping perversely what was not his: Adam lay y-bounden. That wilful graspingness brought genuine loss of life, unavoidable expulsion, alienation, isolation and prolonged absence from felicity. But the Apple Tree in the Song of Songs redeems and recovers these losses. It restores our human presence of mind. Let me enumerate the virtues of this tree. It is impregnated with healing properties; it has spring blossom fecund with possibility; it grows the good fruit which once tasted flushes the whole being to the brim with satisfaction. No wonder St Thomas Aquinas, a little unexpectedly, said the true end of life ought to be the pursuit of happiness: *ut beatus sit.*

Clare and William, I am addressing you by your Christian names, given you at baptism. The liturgy speaks of your espousals as made publicly before 'this congregation'. That means the whole people of God, spreading beyond this particular congregation to include a wider fellowship in space and in time, amongst whom are the dead who would have rejoiced with you and are now remembered. You know in your hearts what you have always known, that your parents and friends bless you and feel themselves blest in you. This congregation of parents and friends stretches out its hands to touch the heads of both of you, as priests do in ordination. This is another such act of hallowing.

The Lord bless you; may love continually attend you; may you possess, and be possessed by, pleasure and happiness; may you never forget or neglect those things which belong to your peace. And may your souls discern the tree of life, laden with fruit and always green.

As the apple tree is among the trees of the wood
So is my beloved among the sons;

His beauty doth all things excel.
By faith I know but ne'er can tell
The glory which I now can see
In Jesus Christ the apple tree.

Commemoration: Donald Davie

> Eye hath not seen nor ear hath not heard ... what things the Lord hath prepared for them that love him.
>
> St Paul's First Epistle to the Corinthians, chapter 2, verse 9.

Let me take the risk of thinking aloud about heaven and its kingdom. After all, people do ask questions about heaven and Christian faith tells a story which affirms life does not end in ultimate extinction.

But what kind of story is it and where does it come from? We need to remember that the ancient Hebrews asked mainly what the Lord required of them in life rather than enquired about immortality. God was the God of the living and at death we returned totally to the elements, ashes to ashes and dust to dust. Grief was not redeemed by promise. And today whether we are Jew or Christian we need to touch those depths of hopelessness before finding any grounds of hope. There is no guilt in grief or in foreboding: 'O spare me a little, that I may recover my strength before I go hence and be no more seen.'

Yet, in the great creative period of the several centuries cradling Christ, there emerged in the various traditions of the one God three strands of hope. Each strand was based on transformation. There was the transformation of earth in the likeness of heaven; of the immortality of the soul; and of the resurrection of the body. The Bible expresses all three: 'Thy kingdom come on earth as it is in heaven'; 'The souls of the righteous are in the hand of God'; and 'This corruptible must put on incorruption.' But that apart, the Bible retains a sublime reticence about the life of heaven, leaving us only with pictures, pointers, metaphors and what Donald Davie called 'sightings'. At the burial of those we love we repeat those pointers with mingled terror and hope, leaving our flowers as mute signs both of the dead of winter and the coming of Spring. Then we return to our still daylight world where clocks tick, buds open and leaves fall. But what of those metaphors, stories, pointers, sightings? Before leaning a little on them, let me follow the sequence of the Bible itself and approach the mystery of life before approaching the mystery of death.

The mystery of human life, of human-ness itself, depends on uncertainty. Uncertainty follows from the interplay within our experience of the orderly and the random. That is why we can always make good retrospective sense of the past, but cannot predict the future except by sketching out more or less likely scenarios. Order is the basis of our capacity to project forward at all; randomness is part of the openness of all our futures. And our humanity actually comes into being because we live at the forward edge of the tension introduced by the movement of time into semi-unknown futures. If we existed enclosed in a pre-determined orderly grid we would revert back from humanity to nature. But with time, uncertainty, anxiety and freedom we enter into an inheritance of changefulness and variability which can include change for the better as well as deterioration. Change for the better and deterioration are impossible without each other and so we live by an ambiguous fusion of terror and promise, gain and loss, miscarriage and birth. (And that was as true of Christ as for ourselves. In prospect redemption itself was exposed to the creative flux of uncertainty. Christ as portrayed in the gospels was uncertain whether it was the appropriate time to make his journey to Jerusalem. Without that uncertainty the good of redemption would have been impossible and the incarnation monstrous.)

So, out of the quivering needle of uncertainty comes all prospect of joy and of preciousness, including the preciousness of life and of our selves. The wonder of our births and the infinite preciousness of a child depend in part on vulnerability and fragility. Humanness is valuable and its extinction very grievous in part because it is endangered. Time, uncertainty and danger make us both grieve for extinction and envisage immortality. We are thereby enabled to think forward about ourselves, either as 'rolled round in earth's diurnal course with rocks and stones and trees' or as immortal creatures 'moving about in worlds not realized'.

And that must mean that uncertainty governs our approach to death as much as our approach to life. There is only the tension of terror and promise. It also means that this time-bound world is not some incidental preparation but an exploration into heaven – and hell – from the moment of birth. The kingdom of heaven is coming continually on earth as it has little to do with eternal rest, but rather with continuous exploration, with seeking for footings, with discovery, freedom and variation.

That is an approach founded on philosophical reflection. But death is approached also in pictures, by pointers, and by 'sightings'. The pictures we possess are lively metaphors drawn from what we *have* already experienced and then throw across a chasm to what is strictly unimaginable. We know, of course, that there is no river flowing out of a heavenly city surrounded by trees for the healing of the nations, any more than there is an undying worm. Nevertheless, we speak of a country 'far beyond the stars' and of a rose that cannot wither. We envisage a city with gracious welcomes, high feastings and safe lodging. And such pictures of fulfilment correspond to a sense of yearning incompleteness in the heart which overlaps a more everyday pursuit of paradise in human love or landscape or home or music. That is why Auden wrote that when he thought of heaven he remembered the murmur of water in limestone country and why Goethe asked the luminous question, 'Do you know the land where the lemon tree blows?'

The trouble is that when we lean too heavily on metaphors they collapse into nonsense. In his poem 'Sunday Morning', Wallace Stevens played with the absurdity of an unchanging heaven, saying that 'death is the mother of beauty'.

> Is there no change of death in paradise?
> Does ripe fruit never fall? Or do the boughs
> Hang always heavy in that perfect sky …

That thought undermines John Donne's moving prayer about 'entering into the house and gate of heaven'. His prayer speaks of a place where there is no darkness nor dazzling but one equal light, and no noise nor silence but one equal music. Light and music are two of the most evocative emblems of heaven but in any serious heaven there would be variability and progression. So there would need to be noise and silence as well as music, brightness and darkness as well as equable light. Pictures and metaphors have their dangers. Yet without them the screen of our imagination dissolves into flashing dots and greyness.

Suppose, then, we lean just a little on our metaphors, our emblems and our stories, what might they say? They seem to say that all promise of heaven is addressed to us personally by name. And if there is a hope, it would have to be like that, since simply to be lost in an ocean of being is only a gentler name for dissolution. The pictures also seem to speak of mutuality, since people exist in relation, and hell has to do with ultimate separateness and total isolation. The picture of a city adorned as for her husband weaves life with mutuality and with love.

Yet all these remain enigmatic, emblematic flowers placed against the door of death to convey both decay and loss, growth and restoration. It remains true that the free creature, to have any possibility at all, must live endangered, totally without guarantees, between abysses of terror and grounds of hope. We are able only to repeat a story which includes the grief and the promise, remembering that the ship of faith carries this mysterious marking that 'the last enemy to be destroyed is death'.

Identification of Quotations

From Richard Rolle and 'The Dream of the Rood' to Charles Sisson, Donald Davie, Jack Clemo, Les Murray, R.S. Thomas and Geoffrey Hill, English poetry can be read as a third testament, and by glancing quotation I have used it that way. Identification and footnotes are as inappropriate and distracting in sermons as they are obligatory in academic texts, and one could even appeal to earlier literary (and musical) practice, for example in Walton's 'Lives', or, for different objectives, 'The Waste Land'. On the other hand where quotation is direct lack of identification can be frustrating, so some identifications are provided instead of an index.

Pages		
8	Christopher Smart	Jubilate Agno
34	Richard Crashaw	A Hymn of the Nativity
62	Christopher Smart	Hymn 11 Easter Day
63	George Herbert	Easter
74	T.S. Eliot	The Rock 10
126	George Herbert	To All Angels and Saints
136	G.M. Hopkins	Carrion Comfort
144	W.H. Auden	Anthem (1945)
158	Les Murray	Poetry and Religion
191	John Dryden	A Song for St. Cecilia's Day
192	Thomas Campion	To Music bent is my retirèd mind
193	W.H. Auden	Anthem for St. Cecilia's Day
104	Les Murray	The Say-But-the Word
		Centurion Attempts a Summary

Glancing and fragmented quotations are indicated here by page and author

11, Hopkins; 15, Eliot; 25, Stevens; 26, Hopkins (twice); 28, Rossetti; 37, Eliot; 38, Hopkins; 43, Watts; 46, Wesley; 47, Wesley; 54, Eliot; 62, Herbert (twice); 66, Donne; 85, Herbert; 96, Keats; 104, Wordsworth; 105, Cowper; 114, Larkin; 117, Blake; 120, Tennyson; 126, Wordsworth; 133, Wordsworth (twice); 148, Hopkins (a collage); 173, Arnold; 179, Lawrence, Sassoon, Wordsworth; 180, Kipling; 192, Auden, Owen, Sassoon, Eliot, O'Shaughnessy; 193, Milton; 195, Donne; 196 Hopkins, Arnold; 197, Yeats; 204, Spenser; 208, Wordsworth (twice); Vaughan.

The section 'Easter: The New Name' deploys an approach used by John Ruskin in *Fors Clavigera.*